ROME TRAVE

2023

Exploring Rome's Rich Heritage and Hidden
Gems:Practical Advice,What to do,What to Eat and
Sightseeing Wonders

Regina E.Todd

1)

TABLE OF CONTENTS

4)

INTRODUCTION TO ROME

Rome's Brief History

Rome, known as the Eternal City, has a fascinating and lengthy history spanning more than 2,500 years. Rome has had a significant impact on the development of Western culture, from its fabled origin through its ascent to become the capital of one of history's greatest empires. Here is a brief synopsis of Rome's key historical eras:

Kingdom's Founding and Period (753–509 BC):
The first monarch of Rome, Romulus, is said to have built it around 753 BC. Before Tarquin the Proud fall in 509 BC, the early Roman Kingdom was controlled by a series of rulers. The Roman Republic officially got underway at this point.

(509 BC – 27 BC) Roman Republic
A time of considerable growth and political progress was the Roman Republic. It was administered by the Senate and elected officials. Rome engaged in a number of battles, founding colonies and forging alliances as it eventually expanded its dominance over the

Italian Peninsula and beyond. During the Republic, renowned individuals like Cicero and Julius Caesar rose to prominence.

Rome's rule from 27 BC until 476 AD:
Under the rule of Augustus, the first emperor, Rome changed from a republic to an empire in 27 BC. Emperor Trajan's reign in the second century AD marked the height of the Roman Empire. It covered a huge area that extended from Syria to Spain and from Britain to Egypt. The empire's many provinces benefited from stability, infrastructural development, and cultural blending.

The Western Roman Empire's Decline and Fall (476 AD):
Numerous difficulties were experienced by the Western Roman Empire, such as political unrest, barbarian tribal invasions, economic woes, and internal strife. The last Roman emperor, Romulus Augustulus, was deposed in 476 AD by the Germanic leader Odoacer. This incident is often seen as the Western Roman Empire's symbolic demise.

(476 AD – 1870) Byzantine Rule and Papal States

The Eastern Roman Empire, often known as the Byzantine Empire, with its capital in Constantinople (present-day Istanbul), prospered as the Western Roman Empire was overthrown. Rome was administered by the Byzantines, and in the eighth century, the Papal States—a theocratic realm ruled by the Pope—emerged.

Papal Influence in the Renaissance (14th–17th centuries):
Rome saw a renaissance of art, culture, and knowledge throughout the Renaissance. Large-scale construction initiatives were commissioned by popes like Julius II and Leo X, who built St. Peter's Basilica and the Sistine Chapel, respectively. Rome developed into a hub of creative brilliance, drawing eminent architects, thinkers, and painters.

19th–20th century Italian Unification and Modern Rome
Italy undertook a process of unification in the 19th century, and in 1871, the newly created Kingdom of Italy chose Rome as its capital. The Victor Emmanuel II Monument and the Via dei Fori Imperiali are only two examples of the new districts and monuments that were built in

7)

the city as a result of tremendous urban expansion.

Rome still serves as a monument to its illustrious history, attracting tourists from all over the globe with its famous buildings, historic sites, and artistic treasures. Not only has the city itself been affected by its past, but also the very underpinnings of Western civilisation.

Location And Climate

Italy's capital city, Rome, is situated on the banks of the Tiber River in the country's central-western region. It is located inside the province of Lazio, 24 kilometers (15 miles) inland from the Tyrrhenian Sea. The city is well-known for both its historical importance as the administrative seat of the old Roman Empire and its scenic location among undulating hills.

Rome has an area of about 1,285 square kilometers (496 square miles). Aventine, Caelian, Capitoline, Esquiline, Palatine, Quirinal, and Viminal are the seven hills that make up the city. These hills, which provide sweeping views of the town, are peppered with old buildings, meandering lanes, and ancient ruin sites.

The city is cut in half by the Tiber River, with the contemporary neighborhoods on the western side and the ancient core on the eastern bank. The two sides of the city are connected by a number of bridges, including the famous Ponte Sant'Angelo and Ponte Milvio.

Rome has a Mediterranean climate with hot, dry summers and warm, rainy winters. Rome's climate has the following salient characteristics:

Summers (June to August): Rome's summers are hot and dry, with average highs of 32°C (79°F) and lows of 26°C (79°F). The hottest months are July and August, when highs sometimes reach 35 °C (95 °F). During the hottest part of the day, it is advised to drink plenty of water and find shade.

Generally favorable seasons in Rome are spring (March to May) and fall (September to November), with moderate temperatures averaging 15°C to 25°C (59°F to 77°F). Because of the pleasant weather and mild rainfall, these seasons are regarded as the best ones for outdoor exploration.

Winter (December to February): Compared to many other European cities, Rome's winters are moderate, with daily highs between 8°C and 14°C (46°F and 57°F). While snowfall is uncommon, this season sees more rainfall. It is advised to wear layers of clothes and a light jacket.

It's crucial to remember that weather conditions might change and that sometimes there could be heat waves or cooler periods. It's a good idea to look at the weather prediction before your trip and prepare appropriately.

The mild winters and extended, sunny summers of Rome's climate make it a popular travel destination all year round. Although the weather is lovely and the city is less congested than during the busiest summer months, spring and fall are often regarded as the ideal times to go.

Cost of Travel

Rome travel expenses might change based on a number of variables, such as the season, your particular travel preferences, and your spending patterns. When calculating the cost of travel to Rome, keep the following important factors in mind:

Flights: Depending on your point of departure, the season, and the airline you pick, the price of flights to Rome will vary. Price changes might be considerable, so it's essential to plan ahead and shop around on several airlines and travel websites to get the best offers.

Rome has a variety of lodging alternatives, from high-end hotels to hostels that are affordable. Prices might change according to the area, facilities, and season. Budget lodgings like hostels or guesthouses may start at around €30 to €60 per night, while a mid-range hotel in a convenient location might cost anywhere from €80 to €150 per night.

Dining: The food of Rome is recognized for being delectable, yet it may be expensive to eat out. Depending on the restaurant's kind, its location, and whether you choose a casual trattoria or an upmarket restaurant, prices might differ. A three-course dinner at a mid range restaurant may run between €25 to €50 per person, while a simple meal in a neighborhood restaurant might cost anything from €10 to €20 per person.

Rome has a comprehensive public transportation network that includes buses, trams, and the metro, all of which are reasonably priced ways to move about the city. For various types of transportation, a single ticket normally costs around €1.50; day tickets and multi-day tourist passes are also offered. Although they might be more costly, there are taxis and ridesharing services like Uber.

Activities & Sightseeing: There are many tourist attractions and historical places in Rome, some of which charge admission. Popular locations like the Colosseum and Vatican Museums charge between €15 to €20 for admission, however costs might vary. To save money, it is a good idea to study attractions beforehand and think about buying a city pass or combo tickets.

Other Expenses: Additional costs to take into account include mementos, shopping, entertainment, and optional guided excursions. Depending on individual tastes and preferences, prices for these might change.

It's crucial to remember that the costs shown here are approximations and may alter depending on variables like seasonality, currency rates, and personal spending preferences. You may anticipate and schedule your costs more accurately by making a budget and doing some pricing research beforehand.

How to get to Rome

Rome, Italy's capital city, may be reached through a variety of modes of transportation. The main routes to Rome are as follows:

By Air:
Leonardo da Vinci-Fiumicino Airport (FCO) and Ciampino-G are the two international airports in Rome. Airport B. Pastine International (CIA). Numerous local and international flights from well-known airlines land at these airports. The main airport is Fiumicino Airport, which is situated around 30 km (18.6 km) southwest of the city center.

Ciampino Airport is a minor airport, and it is located about 15 km (9.3 km) southeast of Rome. There are several ways to get to the city center from the airports, including by rail, bus, taxi, or private transportation.

In a train:
A substantial rail network connects Rome with the rest of Italy and Europe. Roma Termini, which lies in the heart of the city, is the primary railway station in Rome. Major Italian cities including Milan, Florence, Venice, and Naples are easily accessible by high-speed trains like the Frecciarossa and Italo. Rome has international rail service to neighboring nations. If you want a beautiful trip, think about taking the train to Rome and soaking in the beautiful scenery along the route.

By Bus:
Long-distance buses connect a number of European locations with Rome. There are many bus companies that provide affordable choices for passengers, including FlixBus, Eurolines, and Megabus. Rome's bus terminals are often either close to the city's center or adjacent to the city's major railway stations.

By Car:

Rome is accessible by car, and a number of motorways link it to other regions of Italy and Europe. If you're planning to go to Rome by car, be aware that parking in the city center may be difficult and costly, and that traffic can be heavy. It is advised to look up any restricted traffic zones (ZTL) in the city center and be informed of any applicable local traffic laws.

From Cruise
Civitavecchia, the port in Rome, serves as a significant Mediterranean cruise liner hub. If your cruise schedule includes a stop in Rome, you may disembark in Civitavecchia and then take a train, bus, or private conveyance to Rome.

Once you've arrived in Rome, you may utilize the city's extensive public transit system, which includes buses, trams, and the metro, to get about the area and get where you need to go.

To get the cheapest prices and guarantee a hassle-free trip to Rome, it is advised to plan and reserve your transportation well in advance, particularly during busy travel times.

Packing List

It's important to prepare carefully for your vacation to Rome so that you have everything you need and can handle your baggage. A recommended packing list is provided below for your convenience:

Clothing:

Rome requires a lot of walking, so pack supportive footwear that is pleasant to wear.
Pack breathable, light-weight clothing that is appropriate for the destination's climate.
Remember to dress modestly while visiting temples and other holy buildings.
sweater or lightweight jacket: Especially in the spring and fall, evenings may turn chilly.
Travel necessities:

passports and other forms of identification.
Travel adapter: Italy employs plug sockets with a European design, thus one may be required.
Bring some cash in euros with you in case you need to make a little purchase.
Travel insurance: Having travel insurance is usually a good idea in case of unforeseen events.
Bring any required prescriptions, along with some first aid supplies and prescription drugs.

Electronics:

Keep in touch and have access to maps, travel applications, and communication with a mobile phone and charger.
Use your camera to record the breathtaking scenery and journey memories.
Keep your gadgets charged on the road with a power bank.
Miscellaneous:

An umbrella or raincoat is an excellent idea since Rome sometimes experiences rain.
Take a daypack with you while visiting the city so you can have the necessities on hand, such as water, food, and a map.
Use sunscreen and sunglasses to shield yourself from the sun, particularly in the summer.
Keep hydrated while you tour Rome's sights by carrying a reusable water bottle.
Bring your necessary toiletries with you or buy them when you get there.
Keep in mind to check the weather prediction for the dates of your trip and prepare appropriately. Take into account the activities you have scheduled and pack any necessary specialized goods, such as swimwear or formal dress for formal occasions.

Additionally, be mindful of any special guidelines or limitations set out by airlines in relation to the dimensions, weight, and permitted contents of carry-on bags.

You may assure a pleasant and delightful vacation to Rome without being burdened by superfluous goods by packing shrewdly and effectively. Travel safely!

Travel Advice and Rome Etiquette

Dress appropriately: It is polite to wear modest clothing, covering knees and shoulders, while visiting places of worship, such as churches or the Vatican. To respect local traditions, avoid wearing exposing or beachwear apparel in public.

Make careful to validate your tickets at the machines found on buses, trams, and in metro stations if you want to travel in Rome using public transit. If you fail to verify your ticket, inspectors may penalize you.

Pickpockets should be avoided, as in any well-known tourist destination, particularly in busy locations, on public transit, and at well-known sites. Use secure luggage, keep an eye on your possessions, think about wearing a money belt, and store critical papers in hotel safes.

While many Romans can speak English, knowing a few simple Italian expressions like "please," "thank you," and "excuse me" may go a long way in establishing respect and a friendly relationship with locals.

Follow eating etiquette: It is traditional to wait to be seated in restaurants rather than choose a table on your own. Additionally, it's considerate to say "buongiorno" or "buonasera" (good morning or good evening) to the personnel as you arrive. Don't be shocked by the cover fee (coperto), which is often included in table service.

Enjoy the local cuisine: Traditional Roman foods like carbonara pasta, cacio e pepe, and Roman-style pizza are not to be missed as Rome is recognized for its delectable cuisine. Additionally, keep in mind that many restaurants start serving supper about 7 or 8 PM, when Italians generally eat their meal.

Rome is home to a vast number of historical and cultural landmarks. Do not climb or sit on any monuments, statues, or old ruins out of respect for them. To help protect these treasures for future generations, abide by any regulations or instructions offered by the authorities.

Tipping customs: Tipping is not as common in Italy as it is in some other nations, but it is nonetheless customary to leave a little gratuity for excellent service. A normal gratuity is between 5% and 10% of the total cost, or rounding up. Check the bill before adding an extra tip since certain restaurants may include a service fee (servizio incluso) in the total.

Public conduct: Refrain from having loud talks, making excessive noise, or acting disruptively in venues that are open to the public, such as churches and neighborhoods. Remember that Italians appreciate their privacy, so keep your distance while engaging with the populace.

While seeing Rome's famous attractions is a necessity, also take the time to explore the districts outside of the city's major tourist hubs. This enables you to take in the genuine local culture, find undiscovered treasures, and have a more fulfilling vacation experience.

You may have a more pleasurable and courteous trip to Rome by heeding these travel advice and being aware of regional traditions and etiquette.

Best Time to Visit

The ideal time to visit Rome will depend on your choices and the experiences you want to have while there. When deciding when to go, keep the following things in mind:

Rome has a Mediterranean climate, which means that the summers are hot and the winters are pleasant. The spring months of April to June and the fall months of September to October are both popular travel seasons since they often have nice weather and warm temperatures. The hot and congested summer months of July and August are often above 30°C (86°F) in temperature. Compared to many other European cities, the winter season (December to February) is warmer here, although it may still be cold, particularly in January.

Crowds: Rome is a well-liked tourist destination, thus it often has a lot of visitors. Easter, the summer, and the Christmas and New Year holidays are the times of year when the city sees its highest levels of tourism. Consider going in the shoulder seasons of spring and fall when the city is generally less busy if you like to avoid enormous crowds.

Events & Festivals: Throughout the year, Rome holds a number of events and festivals that may enhance your trip by providing a distinctive cultural experience. The Festa della Repubblica (Republic Day) on June 2nd, the Rome Marathon in April, and the Feast of Saints Peter and Paul on June 29th are a few noteworthy occasions. There are important religious rites and festivities held in Rome during the holidays of Christmas and Easter.

Sightseeing and Attractions: During the off-peak seasons, several attractions in Rome could see shorter lines or fewer visitors. Consider going early in the day or getting skip-the-line tickets if you want to visit well-known locations like the Colosseum,

Vatican Museums, or Sistine Chapel to reduce wait periods.

Budget: During the busiest travel times, hotel and airfare costs often increase. Consider traveling during the shoulder seasons or even the winter months if you're seeking for more reasonably priced choices.

The ideal time to visit Rome ultimately relies on your own choices for the weather, people, and events. With moderate weather and fewer tourists, spring (April to June) and fall (September to October) are often regarded as the best seasons to travel. But Rome is charming all year round, and each season has its own special allure.

EXPLORING THE HISTORIC DISTRICT

The Colosseum and Roman Forum

Two famous historical landmarks in Rome that are a must-see for tourists are the Colosseum and Roman Forum. Here are some details about these amazing locations:

Roman Colosseum

The Colosseum, sometimes called the Flavian Amphitheatre, is a historic Roman amphitheater that can be found in the center of Rome. It is regarded as one of the greatest engineering and architectural wonders of the Roman Empire.

History: The Colosseum was a public venue for gladiatorial fights, animal hunts, and other shows that were built in AD 70–80. An estimated 50,000–80,000 spectators might fit there.

The Colosseum is an elliptical-shaped building built of stone and concrete. It has four floors and is decorated with arches and columns. Gladiators, animals, and stage props were kept in its elaborate network of tunnels under the earth, known as the hypogeum.

Visitor advice: To avoid huge lines, get skip-the-line tickets or schedule a guided tour. To learn more about the history and design of the Colosseum, audio tours are available on-site. Be aware that certain places can be off-limits due to preservation or restoration efforts.

The Forum of Rome

The bustling heart of ancient Rome, sometimes referred to as the Forum Romanum, housed the city's political, social, and economic institutions.

The Forum was the center of Roman public life for more than a millennium beginning in the 7th century BC. Important political events, lectures, and religious rites were held there.

The Temple of Saturn, the Arch of Septimius Severus, the Curia (Senate House), the Rostra (stage for speeches), and the Basilica of Maxentius are just a few of the remains and buildings that make up the Roman Forum.

investigation hints: Because the Roman Forum is a large archaeological site, it is advised to set aside enough time for investigation. As it often includes entrance to the Roman Forum and Palatine Hill, think about purchasing a combo ticket that also covers the Colosseum. To better comprehend the historical importance of the place, audio guides and guided excursions are offered.

As UNESCO World Heritage monuments, the Colosseum and Roman Forum provide amazing insights into Roman civilisation. Visitors may go back in time and experience the splendor of the Roman Empire by seeing these sites.

Palatine Hill and the Circus Maximus

Two well-known landmarks in Rome with a strong connection to ancient Roman history are Palatine Hill and the Circus Maximus. These fascinating attractions' details are as follows:

Mount Palatine:

One of Rome's seven hills, Palatine Hill is situated close to the Forum of Rome. Of the seven hills, it is regarded as being the most central and is rich in mythical and historical importance.

History: According to mythology, Rome's founding father, Romulus, founded the city on Palatine Hill in 753 BC. Later, monarchs and nobility coveted it as a place to live. Ruins of palaces, villas, and gardens dating from several eras of Roman history may be seen on the hill.

The majestic Domus Augustana and Domus Flavia, which were formerly lavish homes of Roman emperors, are only two of the imperial palaces whose remains may be seen by tourists. The Farnese Gardens, which are perched atop the hill, provide breathtaking views of the surroundings.

26)

Visitor advice: Tickets that include admission to the Colosseum, Roman Forum, and Palatine Hill are sometimes combination tickets. It is advised to wear comfortable shoes since there are stairs and rough areas to negotiate. To learn more about the historical importance of the location, think about employing an audio guide or going on a guided tour.

Maximus the Circus

In the valley between the Palatine and Aventine Hills stands the ancient Roman chariot racing venue known as the Circus Maximus. In ancient Rome, it was the biggest and most renowned arena.

The Circus Maximus was first utilized for chariot racing, athletic competitions, and public shows in the sixth century BC. It had a lengthy track, a central barrier known as the spina, and enough for nearly 150,000 spectators.

Highlights: Despite being mostly in ruins, the monument nevertheless has its form and provides visitors an impression of the magnificence of ancient Roman entertainment. There is still evidence of the chariot racing course, starting gates, and spectator seating sections.

Exploring Advice: Because the Circus Maximus is a public area, visitors can stroll along the track and take their time exploring the grounds. The site offers panoramic views of the surroundings and informational signs that provide historical context.

Both Palatine Hill and the Circus Maximus give visitors a glimpse of life in ancient Rome and an amazing understanding of the history and magnificence of the Roman Empire. Visitors can fully immerse themselves in Rome's rich cultural heritage by exploring these locations.

Capitoline Hill and Piazza Venezia

Two important sites in Rome are worth visiting: Capitoline Hill and Piazza Venezia. Here is some information on these famous sights:

Congressional Hill

One of Rome's seven hills, Capitoline Hill, also known as Campidoglio, is regarded as the smallest and most significant of the hills. It is close to the Roman Forum and provides breathtaking city views.

Capitoline Hill has played a significant role in Roman history for many years. It served as the political and religious hub of ancient Rome and was home to significant temples and governmental structures. Today, it houses several museums and serves as the administrative center for the city of Rome.

Highlights: Michelangelo created the Capitoline Hill's main square, the Piazza del Campidoglio, in the 16th century. The Marcus Aurelius equestrian statue is at the center of an elegant design. The Capitoline Museums, which are located on the hill and contain an impressive collection of Roman art and artifacts, including well-known pieces like the Capitoline Wolf and the Dying Gaul, are also located there.

Visitor advice: You can reach Capitoline Hill by taking the elevator from the Victor Emmanuel II Monument or by ascending the Cordonata staircase from Piazza d'Aracoeli.

You must pay a separate admission charge for each of the museums on the hill, so plan on spending enough time perusing the offerings and taking in the panoramic views.

Place of Venice

At the base of Capitoline Hill lies a busy area known as Piazza Venezia. It is surrounded by significant monuments and is regarded as Rome's core center.

History: The Palazzo Venezia, a Renaissance mansion that housed the Venetian cardinal in the 15th century, is the source of the square's name. Later, it was used as the Republic of Venice's embassy in Rome.

Highlights: The magnificent Monumento Nazionale a Vittorio Emanuele II, popularly known as the Victor Emmanuel II Monument or Altare della Patria, is the most striking element of Piazza Venezia. This enormous white marble monument celebrates Italy's first monarch and commemorates the unification of the country. For sweeping views of Rome, visitors may ascend to the monument's topmost terrace. In addition, the area serves as a significant transit hub for a number of bus and tram routes that converge here.

Exploration Advice: Take a trip across Piazza Venezia to take in the splendor of the monument and the other buildings. Exercise care while crossing the streets since there is busy traffic in the neighborhood.

Capitoline Hill and Piazza Venezia provide a unique blend of historical importance, stunning architecture, and energetic environment. A fuller knowledge of Rome's lengthy history and its significance as a

30)

political and cultural hub may be gained by exploring these locations.

The Pantheon

In the center of Rome, there stands a magnificent old Roman temple called the Pantheon. Here are some details about this amazing piece of architecture:

The Pantheon is a beautifully preserved temple that was originally constructed as a Roman temple devoted to every Roman deity. Officially known as the Basilica of St. Mary and the Martyrs, it is today used as a church.

History: In 27 BC, during the reign of Augustus, Emperor Marcus Agrippa ordered the construction of the Pantheon. Emperor Hadrian reconstructed the old building between AD 118 and 125 after it was devastated by fire in AD 80. Hadrian's renovation is mostly reflected in the existing structure.

Architecture: The Pantheon's structure is a tribute to the engineering and architectural brilliance of the ancient Romans. The enormous dome, which until recent times was the biggest unreinforced concrete dome in the world, is its most recognizable feature. A round drum that has a portico of Corinthian columns at the entrance supports the dome. The Pantheon's interior is similarly stunning, with an incredible oculus (circular aperture) in the middle of the dome that lets natural light in.

Highlights: The inside of the Pantheon is breathtaking. A feeling of grandeur is produced by the enormous area under the dome, and the mystical mood is heightened by the sunshine flowing through the oculus. The elegant marble floors, subtle embellishments, and harmonic proportions all contribute to the room's overall appeal. The Pantheon houses the graves of several famous people, including Raphael.

Visitor advice: The Pantheon is free to enter, although it may become busy, particularly during the busiest travel times. To avoid crowds, it is advised to attend early in the morning or later in the evening. Keep in mind that the Pantheon is a holy site of devotion and to dress modestly. Be considerate of any ongoing religious events or services occurring within the church.

Attractions close by: The Pantheon's strategic location makes it easy to see nearby attractions. The Spanish Steps, Trevi Fountain, and Piazza Navona are some famous locations close by.

Anyone interested in the history and architecture of the Roman Empire must visit the Pantheon. It is a real wonder of antiquity due to its extraordinary architecture, historical relevance, and spiritual atmosphere.

The Spanish Steps and Piazza di Spagna

The Scalinata di Trinità dei Monti (Spanish Steps) and Piazza di Spagna are well-known attractions in Rome that provide a lovely ambiance and a lively meeting area. These attractions' details are as follows:

Steps in Spanish:

The Trinità dei Monti Church is located at the summit of the Spanish Steps, which rise majestically from Piazza di Spagna. It has 135 stairs and is a well-known gathering spot and social center in Rome.

33)

History: Étienne Gueffier, a diplomat for France, ordered the building of the Spanish Steps in the early 18th century. They were finished in 1725. Francesco de Sanctis and Alessandro Specchi, architects, were responsible for creating the stairs.

Highlights: The Barcaccia Fountain, a lovely fountain designed like a sinking boat, is located at the foot of the Spanish Steps. In the spring, flowers are placed on the stairs itself to create a beautiful scene. You may get a bird's-eye perspective of the city from the top of the stairs.

Exploring Advice: The Spanish Steps may be congested, particularly during the busiest travel times. It's a nice place to relax and observe people or just take in the lively environment. Luxury retail avenues including Via dei Condotti, Via del Babuino, and Via del Corso are nearby.

Spagna Square:

At the foot of the Spanish Steps lies a bustling area known as Piazza di Spagna. The Spanish Embassy to the Holy See, which had a location there in the 17th century, inspired the name of the area.

Highlights: In the early 17th century, Pietro and his son Gian Lorenzo Bernini created the

Fontana della Barcaccia (Fountain of the Old Boat), which serves as the center of attention for the area. Tourists often congregate and cool down at the fountain, which has a boat that is partially submerged.

Exploration advice: Piazza di Spagna is a busy location with plenty of boutiques, stores, and cafés. It's a terrific spot to unwind and take in the bustling scene while enjoying a cup of coffee or gelato. In the holiday season, the area is renowned for its lovely Christmas decorations.

In Rome, the Spanish Steps and Piazza di Spagna are both well-known gathering places and energetic areas. These sites provide amazing experiences for tourists, regardless of their interest in history, architecture, or just the atmosphere of the city.

Trevi Fountain

One of the most well-known fountains in the world, the Trevi Fountain (Fontana di Trevi) is a stunning Baroque masterpiece. Here are some details regarding this famous site:

35)

The Trevi Fountain is a large, elaborate fountain situated in Rome's Trevi neighborhood. Its name, "tre vie," refers to the intersection of three roads where it is located. The magnificent fountain is renowned for its elaborate sculptures and mesmerizing water show.

History: Work of the Trevi Fountain was started in 1732 and finished in 1762. It has sculptures by numerous artists, including Pietro Bracci, and was created by architect Nicola Salvi. To provide water to the surrounding region, the fountain was constructed at the end of the historic Aqua Virgo aqueduct.

The Trevi Fountain's massive proportions and dramatic design define its design and symbolism. A triumphal arch flanked by Corinthian columns serves as the fountain's main focal point. Oceanus, the Roman deity of the sea, is seen above the archway riding a chariot driven by two sea horses, one placid and the other wild. Around the fountain, sculptures and reliefs depict a variety of mythical characters and allegorical themes.

36)

Tradition: Tossing a coin into the Trevi Fountain with your right hand while looking over your left shoulder is a well-known Trevi Fountain custom. It is said that doing so would guarantee your return to Rome. Each day, thousands of people take part in this custom, which collects money that are then donated to charity.

Visitor Advice: Because the Trevi Fountain draws a lot of people throughout the day, it's best to go early in the morning or late in the evening to escape the crowds. When the fountain is lighted at night, a magnificent atmosphere is created, so be prepared for a breathtaking visual experience. As a treasured cultural landmark, the Trevi Fountain deserves your respect.

The area around the Trevi Fountain, which is renowned for its quaint streets, boutiques, and gelaterias, may be explored while you are there. The Pantheon, Piazza Navona, and the Spanish Steps are further close sights.

The Trevi Fountain represents Rome's extensive historical and aesthetic legacy in addition to being a stunning piece of art. It is a must-visit location for those who want to fully experience the magnificence and beauty of the Eternal City.

Piazza Navona

Beautiful Piazza Navona may be found in Rome's ancient center. It is renowned for its alluring Baroque architecture, vibrant ambiance, and lovely fountains. Here are some details regarding this fascinating square:

Piazza Navona is a sizable piazza located on the former location of the Domitian Stadium. In addition to being surrounded by opulent structures, cafés, restaurants, and art galleries, it is also known for its extended oval form.

Piazza Navona's long history began in the first century AD, when it served as a venue for athletic competitions. It changed through time into a public plaza and developed into a bustling center for social events, festivals, and marketplaces.

Stunning Baroque architecture and three prominent fountains may be seen at Piazza Navona.

The Nile, Ganges, Danube, and Rio de la Plata are just a few of the famous rivers that are commemorated in the Fountain of the Four Rivers (Fontana dei Quattro Fiumi), which was created by Gian Lorenzo Bernini.

Giacomo della Porta's statue of a Moor grappling with a dolphin is shown at the Fountain of the Moor (Fontana del Moro), which stands at the southern end of the plaza. Later, Bernini updated it.

Neptune, the Roman deity of the sea, is shown with his trident at the Fountain of the Neptune (Fontana del Nettuno), which is located at the northern end of the plaza. Antonio Della Bitta and Gregorio Zappalà were responsible for its design.

Highlights: Piazza Navona has a lively ambiance and is a busy plaza. Visitors are often amused by street performers, merchants, and musicians. The area also hosts a number of occasions and art exhibits all year long. Also worth seeing is the stunning Baroque Church of Sant'Agnese in Agone, which is located on one side of the Piazza.

Tips for Exploring: Take your time strolling around Piazza Navona and taking in the magnificent fountains, elaborate façade, and little cafés. At one of the outside terraces, you can take in the vibrant atmosphere while enjoying a leisurely lunch or a cup of coffee. Don't forget to bring your camera so you may record the square's splendor.

The Piazza Navona combines history, art, and life in a fascinating way. It is a must-see location in Rome where tourists may take in the energy of this famous piazza and admire its architectural gems.

VATICAN CITY AND RELIGIOUS SITES

St. Peter's Basilica

One of the most well-known and important religious sites in the whole world is St. Peter's Basilica (Basilica di San Pietro). It is situated within Vatican City and is very significant to the Catholic Church. Millions of people come here every year. Here are some details about this stunning basilica:

The biggest Catholic cathedral in the world, St. Peter's Basilica serves as the main place of worship and formal gatherings in Vatican City. It sits on the traditional spot where Saint Peter, one of Jesus Christ's apostles, was buried and is a spectacular example of Renaissance and Baroque architecture.

St. Peter's Basilica was built over the course of more than a century, starting in 1506. Its design included contributions from well-known architects and painters such Donato Bramante, Michelangelo, Carlo Maderno, and Gian Lorenzo Bernini.

The basilica's architecture displays a tasteful fusion of architectural influences. Michelangelo created the basilica's enormous dome, which dominates its façade, as well as the opulent colonnade that surrounds the basilica's entrance area. The expansive interior, magnificent statues, elaborate altars, and complex mosaic artworks astound visitors.

Highlights:

St. Peter's plaza: Bernini created a spectacular colonnade with 284 columns and 88 pillars on the plaza in front of the basilica. An Egyptian obelisk occupies the center and is surrounded by two fountains.

Michelangelo's Pietà, a marble sculpture of the Virgin Mary holding the body of Jesus Christ, is among the most well-known pieces of art in St. Peter's Basilica.

Gian Lorenzo Bernini created the elaborate bronze baldachin that is situated over the main altar. It serves as a cover over Saint Peter's grave.

Climb the Dome: For a stunning perspective of Rome and Vatican City, visitors may go to the pinnacle of the basilica's dome. The ascent entails using stairs or an elevator, then a winding stairway that leads to the summit.

Visitor advice: St. Peter's Basilica is a well-liked destination, thus lengthy lines are frequent, particularly during the busiest travel times. To save time, think about going early in the morning or purchasing a skip-the-line ticket. It is necessary to dress appropriately, with shoulders and knees covered.

Religious Services: As a house of worship, St. Peter's Basilica regularly holds religious events including papal Masses and liturgical celebrations. Depending on the schedule, visitors may be able to attend Mass or see unique religious activities.

Both a powerful spiritual experience and an appreciation for the building's architectural and aesthetic marvels may be had by visiting St. Peter's Basilica. It is a well-known representation of Rome and a tribute to the Catholic Church's long history and steadfast faith.

Vatican Museums

Located in Vatican City, the Vatican Museums (Musei Vaticani) are a veritable gold mine of art and history. They are some of the largest and most well-known museums in the world, displaying an enormous collection of works of art and relics dating back thousands of years. Here are some details on the Vatican Museums:

The Vatican Museums are a collection of galleries and exhibition halls located in Vatican City. Popes throughout the ages have amassed a sizable collection of artwork, sculptures, historical items, and archaeological findings, which are now housed at the museums.

43)

The private collection of Pope Julius II in the early 16th century is where the Vatican Museums got their start. The museums were first opened to the public in the 18th century and have since become a significant cultural institution. Over time, the collection developed via the efforts of succeeding popes, especially Pope Clement XIV, Pope Pius VI, and Pope Pius IX.

Collections: The Vatican Museums are home to a staggering collection of priceless works of art from numerous eras and cultures. Some noteworthy highlights and collections are:

The Sistine Chapel is the gem in the Vatican Museums' crown. The ceiling murals representing events from the Book of Genesis and "The Last Judgment" on the altar wall are among its famous, breathtaking frescoes. Michelangelo's masterwork is also found there.
Raphael Rooms: Raphael and his studio painted these spaces. The Stanze di Raffaello, which showcase beautiful paintings representing mythical and historical subjects, is the centerpiece.
The maps in this collection were ordered by Pope Gregory XIII in the late 16th century, and they are all very detailed.

44)

Mummies, sculptures, and hieroglyphics are among the ancient Egyptian items on display at the Egyptian Museum.
Pinacoteca Vaticana: The Pinacoteca is the Vatican's art museum and is home to a noteworthy collection of works by well-known painters including Caravaggio, Raphael, Leonardo da Vinci, and Titian.
Visitor Advice: The Vatican Museums draw a lot of people, so it's best to reserve tickets ahead of time or choose skip-the-line tickets to avoid lengthy lines. The museums might be overwhelming, so prioritize the exhibits or places you want to see while arranging your visit. There are guided tours and audio guides available for an immersive experience.

Visitors are encouraged to dress modestly, with shoulders and knees covered, since the Vatican Museums are within Vatican City. Keep in mind that taking pictures within the Sistine Chapel is often not permitted.

A fantastic trip through art, culture, and history may be had by visiting the Vatican Museums. The museums provide a comprehensive experience for both art fans and history buffs, from the splendor of the Sistine

Chapel to the interesting Egyptian treasures and Renaissance masterpieces.

Sistine Chapel

One of the most famous and venerated buildings in Vatican City, the Sistine Chapel is known for its stunning paintings. Here are some details regarding this stunning chapel:

The Sistine Chapel is a chapel that may be found within the Vatican Museums. It is an area that is around 40 meters long and 13 meters broad. The chapel has a barrel-vaulted roof and a raised platform for rituals. Its construction is straightforward.

paintings on the Chapel's Ceiling Michelangelo created a beautiful set of paintings on the chapel's ceiling between 1508 and 1512. The most well-known portion is the middle panel, sometimes referred to as the "Creation of Adam," which illustrates the biblical account of God creating Adam. Other episodes from the Book of Genesis are shown on the ceiling as well, including the Creation of Eve, the Fall of Man, and Noah's Ark.

The massive painting "The Last Judgment" by Michelangelo dominates the altar wall of the Sistine Chapel. It depicts the second coming of Christ and the last judgment of sinners and was finished between 1536 and 1541. The painting shows a dramatic arrangement of people, demonstrating Michelangelo's anatomical expertise and intense emotional range.

Conclave and Papal Ceremonies: The Sistine Chapel is essential to how the Catholic Church functions. The papal conclave, which brings together cardinals to choose a new pope, takes place there. Throughout the year, the chapel also holds a number of papal ceremonies and liturgical activities, including as the Papal Mass on significant days.

Visitor Advice: The Sistine Chapel may be congested because to its importance and popularity, particularly during the busiest travel times. To reduce wait times, it is suggested to go early in the morning or get skip-the-line tickets. To protect the hallowed ambience, please respect the severe rules regarding quiet and photography.

47)

Observing the Art: Take your time to savor the frescoes' minute intricacies, vivid hues, and creative brilliance. To obtain a greater grasp of the narratives and symbols reflected in Michelangelo's works, think about employing an audio guide or going on a guided tour.

The Sistine Chapel, which has enormous theological and cultural importance, is a tribute to Michelangelo's exceptional creative genius. Its breathtaking frescoes continue to draw tourists from all over the globe, making it a must-see location for art lovers and those looking to experience the deep grandeur of the Vatican City.

Castel Sant'Angelo

On the right bank of the Tiber River in Rome stands the medieval fortification known as Castel Sant'Angelo, sometimes referred to as the Mausoleum of Hadrian. It is a well-liked tourist destination due to its striking architecture and extensive history. Information about Castel Sant'Angelo is provided below:

History: The 2nd century AD, under the reign of the Roman Emperor Hadrian, marks the beginning of Castel Sant'Angelo rich past. It was first constructed as a tomb for Hadrian and his family and afterwards used as a fortification, a papal palace, and a jail.

The castle's architecture is a fusion of several styles and epochs. The roof of the conical mausoleum construction is capped with a cylindrical drum. The Passetto di Borgo, a fortified passageway linking the castle to Vatican City, was one of several alterations and improvements made to it throughout the years.

The famed Ponte Sant'Angelo (Angel Bridge), which was built by Bernini and his pupils, leads to the castle and is decorated with 10 sculptures of angels. The entryway to the castle is enhanced artistically by these sculptures.

Papal Residence and Museum: During turbulence and danger, the papal residence was Castel Sant'Angelo. The castle's interiors were ornately furnished with lovely paintings, magnificent apartments, and huge halls. The National Museum of Castel Sant'Angelo is located in the castle today and has a collection of works of art, historical items, and military artifacts.

The expansive views of Rome from the balcony are one of the pleasures of a trip to Castel Sant'Angelo. A beautiful view of the metropolis, including the Vatican, the Tiber River, and famous sites like St. Peter's Basilica and the Colosseum, awaits tourists who go to the top of the castle.

Events and Exhibitions: Throughout the year, Castel Sant'Angelo holds a number of gatherings, performances, and short-term displays. The rich history and cultural importance of the castle are further explored via these activities.

A view into Rome's history and a distinctive perspective on the city's architecture may be obtained by visiting Castel Sant'Angelo. The castle is a riveting site for history fans and those looking for panoramic views of Rome due to its advantageous position, stunning architecture, and fascinating historical links.

Basilica di Santa Maria Maggiore

One of Rome's four principal basilicas, the Basilica di Santa Maria Maggiore, often called the Basilica of Saint Mary Major, is devoted to the Virgin Mary. It is a striking church with a noteworthy collection of works of art and a lengthy history. The Basilica of Santa Maria Maggiore is described in the following manner:

History: The Virgin Mary is said to have requested the building of a church at the location where snow would supposedly fall on a hot summer day when she appeared to Pope Liberius and a rich Roman nobleman in a dream in the fourth century. Over the years, the basilica was renovated and enlarged.

Romanesque, Gothic, Renaissance, and Baroque architectural styles may all be seen at the Basilica of Santa Maria Maggiore. The inside displays elegant marble columns, lovely mosaics, and huge chapels, while the outside has a colossal front with elaborate detailing.

Mosaics: The basilica's breathtaking mosaics are among its most prominent characteristics. The main nave's triumphal arch is embellished with a stunning mosaic that features images from both the Old and New Testaments. The

51)

side chapels' mosaics and the apse's mosaics, which portray biblical themes and saints, have elaborate patterns and vivid colors.

Papal Chapel: The basilica is home to the Cappella Sistina, sometimes referred to as the Sistine Chapel of the West and named for Pope Sixtus V. A painted ceiling and walls depicting episodes from the life of the Virgin Mary make this chapel extraordinary.

The Salus Populi Romani, a renowned image of the Virgin Mary, is housed in the Borghese Chapel, another feature of the Basilica di Santa Maria Maggiore. This icon, which is treasured as a miraculous representation, is said to have been painted by St. Luke the Evangelist.

Crypt: The Crypt of the Nativity is located under the basilica's main altar and has a fragment of the manger from Jesus Christ's birth. The crypt is a place of prayer and adoration and is exquisitely ornamented with mosaics.

Visitors may admire the architectural magnificence, historical relevance, and spiritual atmosphere of this extraordinary church by going to the church di Santa Maria

Maggiore. It is a site for devotion, art, and pilgrimage that provides a window into Rome's illustrious religious history.

San Giovanni in Laterano

The Basilica of St. John Lateran, commonly known as San Giovanni in Laterano, is one of Rome's most prominent and notable churches. As the cathedral of the Pope, the Bishop of Rome, it is recognized as the "Mother Church" of the Roman Catholic Church. Listed below are some details regarding San Giovanni in Laterano:

San Giovanni in Laterano is the oldest and tallest of Rome's four main basilicas, which has historical significance. It is regarded as the city's earliest Christian basilica and was dedicated by Pope Sylvester I in 324 AD. Over the years, the basilica has undergone several restorations and alterations.

Romanesque, Gothic, and Baroque architectural elements are beautifully incorporated into the basilica's design. Five entry doors, exquisite carvings, and sculptures of Christ, John the Baptist, and other saints can be seen on the imposing front. The interior has a roomy nave with imposing marble ornamentation, towering columns, and lovely murals.

Holy Stairs: The Scala Sancta, also known as the Holy Stairs, is located next to the basilica. It is said that Jesus ascended these stairs during his Passion from Pontius Pilate's mansion in Jerusalem. Devout pilgrims climb the Holy Stairs on their knees as an act of penance and devotion. It is a well-known pilgrimage destination.

The Lateran Baptistery, one of the oldest still-standing Christian baptisteries in Rome, is part of the basilica complex. It has magnificent mosaics showing scenes from the lives of Christ and John the Baptist, as well as octagonal construction.

San Giovanni in Laterano serves as the Pope's formal seat as the Bishop of Rome. It also houses the papal archbasilica. The Papal Archbasilica is the highest-ranking church in Catholicism, even above St. Peter's Basilica, and it has a privileged position.

The Scala Sancta Chapel, which is located within the basilica, is where the Sancta Sanctorum (Holy of Holies) are kept. The "Acheropita," a representation of Christ, is one of several priceless icons and noteworthy relics that can be seen in the Sancta Sanctorum.

Exploring a location of enormous historical and spiritual significance is made possible by visiting San Giovanni in Laterano. With its stunning architecture, priceless works of art, and strong ties to the pope, it serves as a symbol of the Catholic Church's foundation and power. Romans who are interested in religion and history should both visit the basilica because of its grandeur and religious importance.

Additional Churches and Religious Sites

Rome is well known for its many churches and sacred sites, each of which offers a special fusion of artistic beauty, historical importance, and religious fervor. Here are a few famous temples and places of worship in Rome:

55)

The biggest and most well-known Catholic church in the world is St. Peter's Basilica, which is situated in Vatican City. It is a marvel of Renaissance architecture and is home to important artworks, like Michelangelo's Pietà and the beautiful dome that he planned and Giacomo della Porta finished.

One of the oldest churches in Rome is the Basilica of Santa Maria in Trastevere, which is located in a picturesque area. Its magnificent bell tower, serene plaza, and magnificent mosaics from the 12th century make it a must-see location.

Located close to Piazza del Popolo, the Basilica of Santa Maria del Popolo is renowned for its magnificent collection of artwork, which includes works by Caravaggio, Raphael, and Bernini. Elegant chapels and delicate architectural features embellish the basilica's interior.

The church of San Clemente: Known for its distinct history-layering, this church shows the Roman past under its present-day exterior. A 12th-century basilica that was erected on top of a 4th-century church, which in turn was built on top of a 1st-century Roman home and a Mithraic temple, is open for visitors to explore.

Three outstanding Caravaggio paintings at the Church of San Luigi dei Francesi represent episodes from the life of St. Matthew, and the church is well-known for them. For art lovers, it is a must-see because of the baroque architecture and magnificent artwork.

Church of Santa Maria della Vittoria: This church is a display of Baroque art and is home to Bernini's magnificent work, the Ecstasy of Saint Teresa. It offers a visually appealing experience because of the dramatic sculpture and elaborate interior.

Pantheon: The Pantheon is a major religious monument even though it is not a church in the classic sense. It was formerly a Roman temple before being transformed into a church for Christian worship. The Pantheon's recognizable dome and amazing architectural style never fail to astound.

The catacombs of Rome are historic subterranean cemeteries where early Christians practiced their religion covertly throughout the rule of the Roman Empire. Understanding the early Christian society and its religious customs may be gained by exploring the catacombs.

These are just a handful of the many churches and other places of worship that line the streets of Rome. Whether one is interested in appreciating art, learning about ancient history, or seeking a moment of contemplation and spirituality, each provides a distinctive experience. Visitors may learn more about Rome's extensive religious and cultural legacy by exploring these places.

ROME ART AND CULTURE

Galleria Borghese

A lovely garden in Rome called Villa Borghese Pinciana is home to the Galleria Borghese, an art gallery. It has a vast collection of artwork, sculptures, and artifacts. Here are some details on the Galleria Borghese:

History: The Borghese family, one of Rome's most powerful aristocratic families, founded the Galleria Borghese in 1903 to display their extensive art collection. The collection, which Cardinal Scipione Borghese assembled in the 17th century, contains pieces created by well-known painters of the era.

The gallery has an impressive collection of Renaissance and Baroque artwork. The works of painters like Caravaggio, Bernini, Raphael, Titian, and Canova are on display for visitors to appreciate. The collection consists of decorative arts, sculptures, and paintings, all of which exhibit extraordinary talent.

Sculptures: The Galleria Borghese is known for its sculpture collection, which includes numerous notable pieces. Stunning sculptures by Bernini like "Apollo and Daphne" and "The Rape of Proserpina," which display the artist's ability to convey motion and emotion in marble, are notable artworks.

Paintings: From the 15th to the 18th century, the gallery has a sizable collection of paintings. Among other outstanding pieces, visitors may admire "The Deposition" by Raphael, "David with the Head of Goliath" by Caravaggio, and "Sacred and Profane Love" by Titian.

The Galleria Borghese is located within the spectacular 17th-century Villa Borghese, which is surrounded by verdant grounds. The architecture and interior decor of the house serve as a lovely background for the art collection, resulting in a distinctive and engrossing museum experience.

Visitor Experience: Due to the Galleria Borghese's popularity, it is recommended to purchase tickets in advance since access is restricted to a certain number of people each time slot. This makes your time spent touring the gallery's rooms and admiring the artworks more pleasurable and personal.

Grounds of Villa Borghese: After seeing the museum, spend some time strolling among the lovely grounds that surround the house. The Villa Borghese Gardens provide a peaceful retreat from the busy city with its calm walks, picturesque vistas, and lovely fountains.

Anyone who appreciates art or wants to take in the splendor of Renaissance and Baroque masterpieces should visit the Galleria Borghese. A genuinely unforgettable cultural and visual experience is created in the center of Rome by the marriage of outstanding artwork, superb sculptures, and the lovely setting of the Villa Borghese.

National Roman Museum

The National Roman Museum, or Museo Nazionale Romano as it is called in Italian, is a grouping of four museums in Rome that together display a sizable collection of Roman artifacts and antiquities. Here are some details on the National Roman Museum:

Museums: There are four primary museums that make up the National Roman Museum: the Crypta Balbi, Palazzo Massimo alle Terme, Palazzo Altemps, and the Baths of Diocletian. Every museum presents a distinctive viewpoint on various facets of Roman history and art.

The Palazzo Massimo alle Terme, which is close to the Termini Station, is home to a sizable collection of antiquated Roman artwork and antiques. Magnificent sculptures, frescoes, mosaics, jewelry, and antique coins are on display for visitors to appreciate, offering a thorough overview of Roman creative accomplishments.

Palazzo Altemps: This Renaissance-style palace, which is close to Piazza Navona, is home to a sizable collection of ancient sculptures as well as Greek and Roman artwork. The Galatian Suicide, the Boncompagni-Ludovisi Collection, and the Ludovisi Throne are highlights.

Crypta Balbi: The Crypta Balbi, which is situated in Rome's old center, provides insights into the development of the city through time. It displays archaeological relics, including ancient and medieval buildings and artifacts, to demonstrate Rome's urban growth.

Baths of Diocletian: Housed inside the remains of the ancient Baths of Diocletian, the Baths of Diocletian are the biggest of the four museums. It exhibits a variety of sculptures, pieces of architecture, and antiquities. The epigraphic collection, which displays a vast variety of inscriptions from different historical eras, is another feature of the museum.

Old artwork and antiquities, including sculptures, reliefs, sarcophagi, ceramics, and old Roman jewelry, are on display at the National Roman Museum. The collection provides a window into the customs, ideologies, and aesthetic creations of the Roman Empire.

Temporary exhibits: The National Roman Museum also presents temporary exhibits that explore certain subjects or showcase extraordinary archaeological findings, in addition to its permanent collection. Visitors get the chance to interact with recent findings and study the subject of Roman archaeology via these exhibits.

The National Roman Museum offers a thorough and immersive look into the fascinating history and artistic achievements of ancient Rome. The museum network's extensive collection, dispersed over several sites, provides a thorough grasp of Roman society, making it a must-see for history buffs, archaeology fans, and everyone interested in learning about the ancient world.

(MAXXI) National Museum of 21st Century Arts

A prominent museum of contemporary art, the MAXXI - National Museum of 21st Century

Arts is situated in Rome, Italy, and is devoted to displaying avant-garde pieces of art and architecture from the 21st century. Here are some details on the MAXXI museum:

Architecture: The MAXXI museum building is a stunning example of modern design. Its stunning and cutting-edge form, created by Iraqi-British architect Zaha Hadid, is highlighted by strong geometric shapes, sweeping arcs, and flowing lines. Contemporary art may be shown in a dynamic and interesting area because of the building's distinctive construction.

Collections: The museum has a wide range of contemporary art genres in its collection, including photographs, sculptures, installations, paintings, films, and multimedia pieces. The collection focuses on pieces produced after 2000 that reflect several creative mediums and explore 21st-century issues.

Permanent Collection: The MAXXI's permanent collection is constantly changing and consists of pieces from internationally renowned and up-and-coming artists. The collection presents a variety of creative expressions and viewpoints, reflecting the dynamic and always evolving character of contemporary art.

Temporary exhibits: The MAXXI museum often presents temporary exhibits that include theme presentations, solo exhibitions, and group exhibitions by highly regarded artists from throughout the world. Visitors to these shows get the ability to examine the most recent creative movements, theories, and trends in the contemporary art world.

MAXXI Architecture: The MAXXI features a separate section for architecture in addition to contemporary art. Exhibitions, talks, and seminars on architectural design and its connections to modern culture and society are organized by MAXXI Architecture.

Education and Events: To captivate visitors of all ages and backgrounds, the museum provides educational programs, seminars, and guided tours. A bustling cultural center for creative conversation and exchange, it also conducts a variety of activities, such as live music performances, artist lectures, performances, and film screenings.

MAXXI B.A.S.E. is a room inside the museum devoted to investigation and experimentation. Its full name is Biblioteca degli Artisti, Spazio Espositivo. It supports a vibrant atmosphere for creative production and innovation through hosting artist residencies, workshops, and collaborative initiatives.

You may immerse yourself in contemporary art, learn about cutting-edge creative expressions, and interact with the vibrant cultural environment of the 21st century by going to the MAXXI - National Museum of 21st Century Arts. The MAXXI provides a thrilling and thought-provoking experience in the center of Rome's thriving art scene, whether you're an art fanatic, a fan of architecture, or just inquisitive about the newest creative trends.

Contemporary Art Galleries

Rome boasts a thriving contemporary art scene with several galleries devoted to showing the work of up-and-coming and renowned artists. These prominent galleries for modern art may be found in Rome:

Rome-based Gagosian Gallery: Gagosian is a well-known worldwide gallery with sites all over the globe. In addition to holding exhibits of paintings, sculptures, photographs, and multimedia works, it represents a wide variety of current artists.

The ancient Trastevere area is home to the Lorcan O'Neill Gallery, which features exhibits of modern art and represents both Italian and foreign artists. The gallery's main objective is to present cutting-edge and provocative works in a variety of media.

T293: T293 is a gallery of modern art that is situated in the San Lorenzo district. It displays cutting-edge contemporary art, often showcasing up-and-coming creators who experiment with new creative ideas.

Monitor Gallery: Monitor Gallery is a significant contemporary art venue that supports avant-garde and experimental artistic activities. It features artwork by upcoming and known Italian and international artists, with an emphasis on current creative trends and critical viewpoints.

Frutta: In the Testaccio district, there is a gallery for modern art called Frutta. It offers shows that address social, political, and cultural topics using a variety of creative forms and promotes up-and-coming artists.

MAGMA Gallery: MAGMA Gallery specializes in new media art and contemporary photography. It holds exhibits that feature cutting-edge works by Italian and foreign artists and examine the relationship between technology, society, and creative expression.

Contemporary art gallery Montoro12 is situated in the Monti arts neighborhood. It engages with artists who explore novel media and methods and presents contemporary art in a variety of formats.

Since the 1970s, the Valentina Bonomo Gallery has played a significant role in Rome's contemporary art scene. It sponsors shows that explore conceptual, minimalist, and installation art and represents well-known artists from Italy and beyond.

These are only a few instances of Rome's galleries for modern art. It is possible to connect with current topics and trends, find intriguing new creative voices, and fully immerse oneself in the vibrant world of contemporary art by visiting these galleries. To get the most recent information on exhibits and activities, it's a good idea to visit the galleries' websites or get in touch with them directly. Keep in mind that gallery schedules and featured artists sometimes change.

Opera and Classical Music

Rome has a long history of opera and classical music, and there are many places where you may see unforgettable performances. Here are some noteworthy locations in Rome where you may hear opera and classical music:

The Rome Opera House, commonly known as the Teatro dell'Opera di Roma, is one of the most well-known locations in the city for opera and ballet. It offers a wide variety of ballet performances, as well as classic and modern operas. The opera house is a work of art in terms of architecture and provides a sophisticated environment in which to experience opera.

Accademia Nazionale di Santa Cecilia: One of the oldest musical organizations in the world, the Accademia Nazionale di Santa Cecilia is known for its symphony orchestra and choir. The school presents a range of classical music events, including symphonic and chamber music recitals, with both established performers and up-and-coming artists.

Renzo Piano, a famous architect, created the contemporary and acoustically excellent Auditorium Parco della Musica, a complex devoted to music. The Santa Cecilia Orchestra calls it home, and a variety of classical music events, including symphonic concerts, chamber music, and solo recitals, are presented in its three concert rooms.

Rome Chamber Music Festival: Held yearly in the city, this festival was started by famous pianist Sir Antonio Pappano. The festival draws top artists from across the globe who collaborate to play chamber music in small settings, giving spectators a close-up and personal encounter with the music.

Concerts at churches: Rome is recognized for its stunning churches, and many of them hold classical music performances all year long. For performances of sacred music and classical works, churches like Sant'Ivo alla Sapienza, Sant'Agnese in Agone, and Chiesa di Sant'Alessio all'Aventino provide breathtaking settings.

performances at Villa Medici: The French Academy in Rome, Villa Medici, hosts a number of performances that include both classical and modern music. The concerts are held in the villa's stunning grounds, which provide a distinctive and lovely atmosphere for listening to music.

Rome features a number of music events every year that include opera and classical music. A broad variety of acts are presented at various locations across the city during festivals including Roma Opera Omnia, Estate Romana, and RomaEuropa Festival.

A classical music concert or opera performance in Rome gives you the chance to experience the city's rich cultural legacy and take in its timeless beauty. Experience the rich musical legacy of Rome, whether it be in a huge opera theater, a little concert hall, or an ancient cathedral. It is a delight for music lovers and a special feature of any trip to the city.

Roman Theaters and Cinemas

Rome boasts a vibrant theater and film culture with a variety of places to see live acts and movies. These famous Roman theaters and cinemas are listed below:

The Teatro di Marcello, sometimes referred to as the Theater of Marcellus, is a historic Roman theater that can be found in Rome. Despite being abandoned as a theater, its remains are a well-liked tourist destination. In the summer, the theater sometimes holds outside performances and festivals.

The Teatro dell'Opera di Roma is the city's primary opera house, as was already noted. It also sometimes performs theatrical productions, bringing both classic and modern plays to the stage, in addition to opera and ballet performances.

Teatro Argentina: Operative since the 18th century, Teatro Argentina is a renowned theater in Rome. It features a variety of plays, musicals, and experimental theater pieces from both the classical and contemporary eras. The venue has a long history and has hosted several renowned writers and performers.

Theater Quirino: The theater Teatro Quirino is close to Piazza Venezia. It offers a varied schedule of theatrical productions, including comedies, musicals, and dramas. The theater often presents both Italian and foreign performances that represent a range of dramatic styles and genres.

Cinema Barberini: The ancient Rome movie theater known as Cinema Barberini shows both popular and indie films. It has many screens and presents special events, retrospectives, and film festivals. The theater is a well-liked option for moviegoers due to its lovely atmosphere and convenient location.

Cinema Nuovo Olimpia: Another well-known movie theater in Rome is Cinema Nuovo Olimpia. It shows a variety of movies, including new releases from throughout the world, independent films, and retrospectives of great films. In addition, the theater periodically conducts film-related activities including Q&A sessions with directors and actors.

Cinema Farnese is a distinctive theater housed in a historic structure close to Campo de' Fiori. In a historical atmosphere, it provides a mix of recent blockbusters and vintage movies. The theater has a unique atmosphere and is renowned for its plush seats and superior sound quality.

The theaters and movie theaters in Rome are only a few examples. Rome provides a range of locations where you may indulge in the arts and enjoy entertainment in a city famed for its cultural legacy, whether you're interested in seeing live theatrical performances or the newest movies.

Events and Festivals

Every year, Rome celebrates a number of festivals and events to honor the arts, culture, music, gastronomy, and more. Here are some of Rome's significant celebrations and occasions:

The International Rome Film Festival, often referred to as the Rome Film Festival, is held each year in October. It features a broad variety of premieres, retrospectives, and foreign films. Renowned directors, actors, and business leaders from all around the globe attend the festival.

Estate Romana, or "Roman Summer," is a term used to describe a number of festivals and cultural activities that take place in Rome during the summer. It consists of outdoor theatrical productions, movie screenings, art exhibits, and culinary festivals hosted at different venues across the city.

Carnevale Romano: The carnival season, which is celebrated in February, is known as Carnevale Romano in Rome. With vibrant parades, masked processions, street entertainment, and celebrations, the city comes to life. It's a joyful time when residents and guests may participate in the fun and enjoy the energetic carnival atmosphere.

Festa della Repubblica: Held on June 2nd, this holiday honors the founding of the Italian Republic. A military parade is staged along Via dei Fori Imperiali to commemorate the occasion, and a formal ceremony is performed at the Altare della Patria. It's a patriotic event that highlights the history and culture of Italy.

Roma Europa Festival: From September through December each year, the Roma Europa Festival is a diverse arts event. It offers a varied schedule of performances in the performing arts, visual arts, music, and multimedia works. The festival promotes intercultural communication by showcasing modern creative forms.

The Rome Jazz Festival is a significant gathering for jazz fans and features prominent local, national, and worldwide jazz performers. The festival includes a number of performances, jam sessions, and seminars honoring the genre at different locations across the city.

Taste of Roma is a food event that highlights the greatest dishes from Rome's restaurant industry. The event, which takes place in September, brings together well-known chefs, eateries, and culinary artists. Visitors may participate in seminars, culinary demonstrations, tastings, and samplings of a broad range of mouthwatering foods and regional delicacies.

White Night (Notte Bianca) is a yearly celebration in September during which the city remains awake all night long. Special events, exhibits, live performances, and entertainment are all available late into the night in museums, galleries, stores, and historical locations. It's a chance to take in Rome's cultural riches in a distinctive and lively setting.

Among the many festivals and events held in Rome, here are just a few examples. There is always something fascinating to enjoy when visiting since the city's calendar is packed with a variety of holidays, cultural events, and creative exhibitions. It's a good idea to double-check each event's precise dates and information in advance since they could change from year to year.

PARKS GARDENS AND OUTDOOR SPACES

Villa Borghese

A lovely park with an area of around 80 hectares, Villa Borghese is situated in the center of Rome. It is one of the biggest municipal parks and provides a peaceful haven away from the busy streets. What to anticipate from Villa Borghese is as follows:

The park is renowned for its perfectly maintained gardens, verdant greenery, and picturesque scenery. You may relax on the lawns, take a walk along tree-lined paths, or hire bicycles to ride throughout the park's expansive grounds. Numerous plant species, including exotic trees, flowers, and fountains, may be seen in the gardens.

Galleria Borghese: Located within Villa Borghese, this famous art gallery is home to an amazing collection of sculptures, paintings, and artifacts. Masterworks by well-known painters including Bernini, Caravaggio, Raphael, and Titian may be found in the gallery. Since the gallery only allows a set number of people in at once, it is preferable to reserve tickets in advance.

Pincio Terrace: The Pincio Terrace, which is at the summit of Pincian Hill, provides a sweeping vista of Rome's cityscape. You may get amazing views of famous places like Piazza del Popolo, the Vatican City, and the Roman roofs from this location. It's a well-liked location for taking beautiful sunset pictures.

The French Academy in Rome is housed in the famous Renaissance mansion known as mansion Medici, which is located within the park. Although the home itself is not usually accessible to the public, its gardens may be seen on certain days and at certain hours. The villa's grounds give a peaceful haven and a chance to admire its exquisite architectural design.

Bioparco: The Rome zoo, Bioparco, is located in Villa Borghese. With a diverse collection of animal species from throughout the globe, it is a well-liked attraction for families and animal enthusiasts. The zoo gives visitors of all ages a fun and enlightening experience by emphasizing conservation initiatives and education.

The Museo Carlo Bilotti displays modern art, including paintings and sculptures, in the space that was formerly the Villa Borghese Orangery. Temporary exhibits with various creative expressions and viewpoints are often held at the museum.

Recreational opportunities: Villa Borghese provides guests with a range of recreational opportunities. Play tennis or soccer, hire a rowboat and paddle around the lake, or go to the Silvano Toti Globe Theatre, an outdoor theater that puts on shows in the summer.

In the midst of the hectic metropolis of Rome, Villa Borghese is a popular destination for both residents and visitors. A trip to Villa Borghese is a must-do activity while you are in Rome, regardless of whether you are interested in art, nature, or just unwinding in a serene environment.

Villa Doria Pamphili

A sizable park called Villa Pamphili, commonly referred to as Villa Doria Pamphili, is situated in Rome's western region. It is one of the city's biggest manicured public parks, spanning more than 180 hectares. What can you discover and take pleasure in at Villa Doria Pamphili?

Large-scale gardens with sloping hills, meadows, and tree-lined walks may be found in the park. It provides a serene and natural setting perfect for relaxing hikes, picnics, and other activities. You may stroll around the park's rich vegetation, ogle the immaculate lawns, and take in the tranquil environment.

home Pamphili: In the center of the park, there is a historic home called Villa Pamphili that previously belonged to the wealthy Pamphili family. You may still admire the villa's external architecture and wander around the surrounding grounds even though it is privately owned and not accessible to the general public.

Lake and Fountains: Villa Doria Pamphili has a lovely lake with rowboat rentals available for a relaxing trip on the water. A number of fountains may also be seen dotted about the park, contributing to its tranquil atmosphere while offering a refreshing sight.

Sports and Playgrounds: The park provides a range of recreational amenities to guests of all ages. There are kid-friendly playgrounds with swings, slides, and climbing frames. In addition, there are tennis courts and sports grounds where you may play outdoor sports like tennis, basketball, and soccer.

Jogging and Cycling: Villa Doria Pamphili is a well-liked location for jogging and cycling due to its numerous trails and wide-open areas. You may take advantage of the park's natural splendor by going for a picturesque run or bike ride.

Giardino dei Melangoli: The Giardino dei Melangoli is a lovely garden with citrus trees that is part of Villa Pamphili. You may have a leisurely walk there in a serene environment while taking in the aromatic citrus orchards.

Events and Festivals: Throughout the year, Villa Doria Pamphili holds a few concerts, events, and cultural festivals. With live music, performances, and festivities, these occasions animate the park and give guests a taste of its distinctive and energetic atmosphere.

Rome's Villa Doria Pamphili is a hidden treasure that provides a tranquil haven from the bustle of the city. It offers many possibilities to appreciate the peacefulness of the surroundings, interact with nature, and participate in outdoor activities. A trip to Villa Doria Pamphili is a joy whether you're looking for a peaceful stroll, a family adventure, or a place to relax among nature.

Appian Way Regional Park

The Parco Regionale dell'Appia Antica, often known as the Appian Way Regional Park, is a beautiful and historic park situated on the southern suburbs of Rome. One of the most notable and well-preserved old Roman routes, the Appian Way, is a substantial component of what it includes. Here are some things you may learn and do at the Appian Way Regional Park:

The Appian Way, a route constructed in 312 BC that linked Rome to the southern regions of Italy, is preserved in part in the park. You may immerse yourself in history by strolling or bicycling along this historic route as you pass past old Roman graves, ruins, and monuments. As you tour the well-preserved archaeological ruins, you may try to picture what life was like during the Roman Empire.

Catacombs: The park is well-known for its catacombs, which were early Christian and Jewish communities' subterranean cemeteries. San Callisto, San Sebastiano, and Domitilla Catacombs are a few of the park's most famous catacombs. There are guided tours available that provide information about the intriguing history and spiritual importance of these subterranean graveyards.

Natural beauty may be found in plenty in the Appian Way Regional Park, which also has a wealth of historical monuments. The park has beautiful scenery, wide open areas, and rural portions. You may take leisurely strolls, have a picnic, or just take in the tranquil settings away from the bustle of the city.

Villas and Ruins: There are several old Roman villas and ruins scattered around the area. The splendor and wealth of ancient Roman life may be seen in these archaeological sites. The Circus of Maxentius, Villa di Massenzio, and Villa dei Quintili are notable locations. You may admire the architectural accomplishments of the past by exploring these ruins.

Cycling and recreation: Because of its historical importance and attractive paths, bikers enjoy the park. Renting a bicycle is an excellent way to see the park's historic sites and scenic landscape. You can then follow the authorized cycling pathways that loop through the area. The park also has locations for picnics, leisure, and entertainment.

Cultural concerts, exhibits, and activities are periodically held in the Appian Way Regional Park. These activities provide a chance to take in a lively environment while learning more about the region's history and cultural heritage.

You may go back in time and see the remains of ancient Rome by visiting the Appian Way Regional Park. It's an opportunity to discover historical sites, take in the scenery, and comprehend the importance of this recognizable route. A trip to the Appian Way Regional Park is a special and educational experience, regardless of your interests in history, ecology, or outdoor recreation.

Janiculum Hill

85)

One of Rome's seven hills, Janiculum Hill, also called Gianicolo, provides breathtaking views of the city. Janiculum Hill, which stands on the western bank of the Tiber River, is significant both historically and culturally. What you may find and do on Janiculum Hill is as follows:

Panoramic Views & Viewpoints: Janiculum Hill offers stunning panoramic views of Rome's skyline. You may take in expansive views of the ancient city center from the hill's high viewing points, including sights like St. Peter's Basilica, the Vatican City, the Tiber River, and the Roman roofs. When the city is bathed in a golden light at sunset, it is the greatest time to come.

The equestrian monument of Giuseppe Garibaldi, a well-known Italian commander and important player in the country's unification, is one of the noteworthy sights on Janiculum Hill. Garibaldi and his contributions to Italian history are honored by the monument. You may get a dominating view of the city from this location.

Fontana dell'Acqua Paola: The Fontana dell'Acqua Paola, often referred to as the Fontanone, is a majestic fountain that dates back to the 17th century and is situated at the summit of Janiculum Hill. The fountain has a striking façade embellished with reliefs and figurines. Both residents and tourists use this popular location to unwind and enjoy the natural surroundings.

The Janiculum Terrace is a large observation platform with seats where you may rest and take in the panoramic views, and it is close to the Fontana dell'Acqua Paola. It's a peaceful place to unwind, have a picnic, or just take in the splendor of Rome as it unfolds in front of you.

Historical Significance: Janiculum Hill is significant because it was instrumental in defending Rome throughout history during several battles. During the 1849 defense of the Roman Republic against French forces, it served as a crucial location. The hill's cultural and historical value is increased by the many plaques, monuments, and historical markers that record these events.

Janiculum Hill is a great place for leisurely hikes and getting close to nature. The hill's abundant vegetation, which includes parks and trees, provides a tranquil haven away from the hectic metropolis below. You may have a leisurely walk along the trails, take in the serene surroundings, and notice how peaceful the hill is.

With its combination of history, the natural world, and breathtaking vistas, Janiculum Hill provides a unique viewpoint on Rome. A trip to Janiculum Hill is strongly advised whether you're into history, photography, or just want to relax.

Orto Botanico (Botanical Garden)

In the center of Rome, there is a tranquil retreat called Orto Botanico, sometimes referred to as the Botanical Garden. With roots in the 16th century, it is one of Europe's oldest botanical gardens. What you may discover and do in the Orto Botanico is as follows:

Botanical Diversity: A wide variety of plant species from all over the globe may be found at the Botanical Garden. You'll come across a broad range of flora, including rare species, tall trees, fragrant herbs, and exotic flowers as you meander along its well-kept trails. The garden is the perfect location for plant aficionados and outdoor enthusiasts as it doubles as a living museum of botanical variety.

Old Buildings: The garden has a number of old buildings that contribute to its attractiveness. Renaissance architecture is well shown in the center structure, also known as the Casina del Cardinale, which was constructed in the 16th century. The park also has a Japanese park, a small pond, and other sculptures that add to its visual appeal.

Plants that are Medicinal and Aromatic: Orto Botanico offers a section just for plants that are Medicinal and Aromatic. Various plants and herbs that are used in cooking and for healing purposes are shown here. Visitors get the chance to learn about the customary usage of these plants, as well as their significance in traditional medicine and cuisine.

Facilities for Education and Research: The Botanical Garden is a place for education and research. For botanical study and research, it has labs, classrooms, and libraries. Additionally, it provides visitors with information on plant biology, conservation, and environmental sustainability via educational programs, guided tours, and seminars.

Recreation & Relaxation: The garden offers a peaceful setting for guests to rest and rejuvenate among nature. The garden has chairs and shady spots where you may relax, read a book, or have a picnic. It's the ideal location for a tranquil break away from the hectic metropolis.

Events & exhibits: Throughout the year, Orto Botanico conducts a number of events, exhibits, and cultural activities. These occasions include live music concerts, photographic exhibits, and art installations. They provide a chance to interact with the botanical world from a new angle and take in the beauty of the garden in a unique manner.

You may experience the marvels of plant life and get fully immersed in the splendor of nature by going to Orto Botanico. A trip to the Botanical Garden is a lovely and educational experience, whether you're interested in botany, looking for a peaceful place to unwind, or just want to see another side of Rome.

Tiber River Walk

The Tiber River Walk is an enjoyable opportunity to see Rome while taking in the natural splendor and peaceful atmosphere of the Tiber River. Here are some things you may do and see along the Tiber River Walk:

Walkways along the river: The Tiber River Walk has well-kept walkways that follow the river and provide a nice route for bikers, runners, and walkers. You may take a leisurely walk down the riverfront and enjoy the tranquil setting, views of the river, and surrounding urban landscape.

Historic Bridges: Along the Tiber River, there are a number of recognizable bridges that are worth investigating when out for a stroll. The Ponte Sant'Angelo, Ponte Sisto, Ponte Fabricio (also known as the Bridge of Four Heads), and Ponte Milvio are a few of the well-known bridges. These bridges not only have stunning architecture but also have historical value and give magnificent river views.

Riverfront Attractions: Along the Tiber, you'll pass by a number of attractions and sites. Historical structures including Castel Sant'Angelo, Palazzo di Giustizia, and Santa Maria in Trastevere are scattered along the riverbed. Take your time to savor the architectural wonders and discover their importance in terms of history and culture.

Outdoor Cafés and Restaurants: There are several outdoor cafés, bars, and restaurants with riverbank seating along the Tiber River Walk. These places provide a relaxing environment for people to relax, taste Italian food, and sip cool beverages while gazing out over the river. It's a perfect chance to have a leisurely dinner or a cup of coffee while taking in the riverbank ambiance.

Tiber Island: A distinctive and endearing island situated in the midst of the river, Tiber Island is accessible via the Tiber River Walk. The island, which is connected by two old bridges, is renowned for its historical value and its medical facilities. You may stroll about the island, go to the San Bartolomeo all'Isola Basilica, and take in its unique beauty.

Street Art and Cultural Events: The Tiber River Walk often provides a setting for cultural events, outdoor plays, and street art exhibits. Vibrant murals, art works, or street performers exhibiting their skills could be encountered. Be on the lookout for these vibrant creative displays that enhance the riverbank stroll.

The Tiber River Walk has a wonderful atmosphere, especially in the nights when the river is exquisitely lighted. It is a well-liked location for couples to take a romantic walk or partake in a romantic supper along the river because of the romantic ambiance created by the mellow glow of the street lights reflecting on the water.

Rome may be explored in a charming and peaceful manner along the Tiber River Walk, which offers a variety of scenic views, historical sites, and cultural activities. A stroll along the Tiber River is a must-do while you are in Rome, regardless of whether you want to find some peace and quiet, get some exercise, or find a romantic backdrop.

Beaches Close to Rome

93)

Rome is not situated exactly on the shore, but there are a number of stunning beaches close by. Here are several beaches you may visit close to Rome to unwind by the water:

The nearest beach to Rome is Ostia Beach, which is located in the town of Ostia and is about 30 kilometers to the southwest of the capital. It has a considerable amount of sandy beachfront and is conveniently close to public transit. Along the shore, there are several beach clubs and amenities where you may hire umbrellas, loungers, and take advantage of seaside food choices.

Fregene Beach is a well-liked vacation spot for both residents and visitors. It is located about 25 kilometers northwest of Rome. It has a sizable sandy beach and crystal-clear seas. The bustling ambiance, hip beach clubs, and beachfront restaurants offering delectable seafood specialties make Fregene a popular vacation destination.

Santa Marinella: Santa Marinella is a gorgeous coastal hamlet with a long, sandy beach that is located about 60 kilometers northwest of Rome. There are both open spaces and exclusive beach clubs available at the beach. Santa Marinella is renowned for its clean seas and welcoming environment for families.

Sabaudia Beach: This unspoiled natural environment is located around 90 kilometers southeast of Rome and is a part of the Circeo National Park. The beach is renowned for its serene atmosphere, gentle sand dunes, and crystal-clear seas. If you're seeking for a more isolated and pristine beach experience, this is a fantastic choice.

130 kilometers southeast of Rome lies Sperlonga Beach, which is well-known for its gorgeous shoreline and blue waves. The beach has both sandy sections and rocky coves and is surrounded by rocks. Sperlonga is the ideal place to experience both natural beauty and cultural discovery since it is a lovely seaside town with a gorgeous medieval core.

Anzio Beach is a well-liked vacation spot for both residents and visitors. It is located around 60 kilometers south of Rome. The beach has a variety of rocky and sandy regions, as well as a number of beach clubs and amenities. You may discover more about Anzio's past by visiting the Anzio War Cemetery and the Museum of the

Landing. Anzio is also noted for its historical importance as the location of the Allied landing during World War II.

These beaches close to Rome provide a welcome respite from the bustle of the city, enabling you to unwind, soak up the sun, and take in the Mediterranean coastline. There is a beach close to Rome that will fit your tastes, whether you like a bustling beach with services or a more remote beach with a natural backdrop.

CULINARY DELIGHTS IN ROME

Popular Regional Cuisines And Eateries

You may savor a range of delectable regional specialties that highlight the city's gastronomic history when visiting Rome. Following are some of the most well-known Roman cuisine and the best places to enjoy them:

The Pecorino Romano cheese, pancetta, eggs, and black pepper that go into making the traditional pasta dish carbonara in Rome. The pasta is wonderfully coated with the creamy, rich sauce. Genuine Carbonara may be found at Trattoria da Danilo and Roscioli, which are both highly recommended.

Cacio e Pepe, which translates to "cheese and pepper," is another well-liked pasta dish that combines spaghetti, Pecorino Romano cheese, and black pepper. Flavio al Velavevodetto or Roma Sparita are the places to go for a fantastic Cacio e Pepe experience.

Pizza made in the Roman style is distinguished by having a thin, crunchy crust. Numerous pizzerias can be found all across the city, but Pizzarium and Da Remo are well known for their outstanding Roman-style pizza.

Suppl: In Rome, these deep-fried rice balls are a favorite fast food item. Usually, they are covered with breadcrumbs, packed with mozzarella and ragù sauce. Visit Trapizzino or Supplizio and sample their delectable Suppl.

A Roman-style meal known as saltimbocca alla romana is created with prosciutto, fresh sage, and delicate veal that has been braised in butter. The Saltimbocca alla Romana at

Checchino dal 1887 and Trattoria Monti is amazing.

Roman Jewish Cuisine: There is a strong Jewish culinary legacy in Rome, and dishes like Bucatini all'Amatriciana (pasta with tomato sauce and guanciale) and Carciofi alla Giudia (fried artichokes) are deserving of a taste. Visit Nonna Betta or Giggetto al Portico d'Ottavia for real Roman Jewish food.

Gelato: Without indulging in some delectable gelato, a vacation to Rome would not be complete. Famous for their extensive flavor selections and premium gelato, Gelateria La Romana and Gelateria Fatamorgana are two gelaterias.

Rome's street food culture is a great place to get a fast snack. Mordi e Vai at the Testaccio Market is a great place to get a snack or a delectable panino. Don't forget to try one of Er Buchetto or Panificio Bonci's well-known porchetta sandwiches.

Keep in mind that there are other outstanding eating alternatives in Rome; these are just a few favorites. Even more undiscovered treasures and gastronomic pleasures may be found by exploring nearby areas like Trastevere, Testaccio, and Monti. Good appetite!

Coffee Culture and Cafes

Rome has a thriving coffee culture that permeates every aspect of everyday life. Italians take their coffee very seriously, thus the city is full with quaint cafés and coffee bars. Here are some details on Rome's coffee culture and some suggestions on where to sample it:

Romans begin their days with a fast dose of espresso, the robust and concentrated coffee that is the cornerstone of Italian coffee culture. Any café or coffee shop where you may, get an espresso, stand at the counter, and enjoy the robust taste. Outstanding espresso is served in the famed historic cafés Sant'Eustachio Il Caffè and Tazza d'Oro.

Cappuccino: In Rome, cappuccinos are often drank for breakfast and after 11am Espresso, steaming milk, and a fluffy foam topping are all included. At Antico Caffè Greco or Bar del Fico, have a classic cappuccino with a hot croissant.

Romans are known for their delicious coffee beverage known as the Marocchino. Espresso, steaming milk, and a little sprinkling of cocoa powder combine to make this delightful and fragrant drink. Visit Ciampini or Roscioli Caffè Pasticceria and order a Marocchino.

Granita di Caffè: Romans like a cold Granita di Caffè during the sweltering summer months. It's a coffee granita dessert with whipped cream that is semi-frozen. Excellent Granita di Caffè may be found in Bar Sant'Ambrogio and Gelateria del Teatro.

Coffee & Pastries: Enjoying a cup of coffee while munching on an authentic Italian pastry. For a large assortment of freshly made pastries and pastries, head to Pasticceria Regoli or Roscioli Caffè Pasticceria.

Coffee Roasteries: Rome offers several excellent coffee roasters for coffee lovers interested in learning more about the preparation of coffee. Visit Caffe Sant'Eustachio or Roscioli Caffè Pasticceria for a glimpse inside the process of coffee roasting and a chance to sample freshly roasted beans.

Historic cafés: There are several old cafés in Rome that have been selling coffee for years. These coffee shops give a look into the history of the city and have a distinctive atmosphere. Take in the ambiance and a cup of coffee at Antico Caffè Greco, Caffè Sant'Eustachio, or Caffè Canova Tadolini.

Always remember to sip your coffee leisurely, stand at the counter like the natives, and take in the tastes and scents to really experience the Italian coffee culture. Rome's café culture provides a lovely and genuine coffee experience, regardless of whether you want a traditional espresso or wish to try the Roman coffee specialty.

Gelato and Desserts

Rome has a delicious selection of sweets to sate your sweet tooth when it comes to gelato and desserts. Here are several dessert places and gelaterias in Rome that you must visit:

Gelateria Fatamorgana: This establishment, well-known for its inventive and artisanal gelato flavors, provides a variety of mouthwateringly different and tasty choices. You'll find something to tempt your taste buds, from traditional tastes like pistachio and stracciatella to creative mashups like lavender and white chocolate with basil.

Gelateria del Teatro: This shop is well-known for its premium gelato, which is created using local, seasonal ingredients. They offer alternatives including ricotta and fig, white chocolate with rosemary, and strawberry with balsamic vinegar, which vary from classic to innovative tastes. The "Gelato del Teatro," their hallmark taste, is a wonderful mashup of hazelnut, chocolate, and biscuits.

Il Gelato di San Crispino: A famous gelateria noted for its focus on simplicity and quality, Il Gelato di San Crispino is situated close to the Trevi Fountain. Their gelato has a smooth, creamy texture and is created with natural ingredients. Try some of their well-known varieties, such as the traditional Fior di Latte and honey.

Pasticceria De Bellis: This storied pastry business in the Prati district is a dessert lover's dream come true. Enjoy a variety of cannoli, sfogliatelle, tiramisu, and other Italian pastries, cakes, and biscuits. They also provide a beautiful variety of macarons, chocolates, and authentic Roman sweets.

The "Tiramisu King," Pompi, is a well-known dessert shop that specializes in tiramisu. Their tiramisu is offered in a variety of flavors, including traditional and pistachio.

Enoteches and Wine Bars

Rome is a great city for wine enthusiasts since it has a variety of wine bars and enoteche (wine stores) where you can enjoy and learn about the world of Italian wines. Here are some suggested enoteche and wine bars in Rome:

Enoteca Corsi is a charming wine bar and store with a large range of Italian wines that is situated in the Trastevere area of Rome. You may buy a bottle of wine to drink on site or take home or experience a range of wines by the glass.

Cul de Sac: This well-liked wine bar, which is close to Piazza Navona, is renowned for its large wine selection, which has more than

1,500 labels. They concentrate on local and small-production wineries and specialize in Italian wines. For a great tasting experience, serve your wine with a variety of cheese and cold meats.

Trimani Wine Bar: Trimani is a well-known brand in Rome's wine sector, and their wine bar is a fantastic location to learn about Italian wines. They are close to Termini Station and provide a wide range of wines, including vintage and unusual bottles. The educated staff can assist you navigate the wine selection and choose the ideal bottle.

Il Goccetto is a delightful wine bar with a warm, homey atmosphere that is tucked away in the core of Rome's old district. With a carefully chosen collection of Italian and foreign brands, they specialize in natural and biodynamic wines. Enjoy their excellent range of cheese and cured meats with a glass of wine.

While largely renowned for its gourmet deli and restaurant, Roscioli Salumeria con Cucina also offers a wonderful wine list with a broad selection of Italian wines. Whether you're ordering a variety of Italian cheeses, cold cuts, or their world-famous carbonara, the experienced sommeliers can suggest the ideal wine to go with your meal.

Wine lovers seeking a distinctive tasting experience should definitely choose Rimessa Roscioli, a wine bar and restaurant. Wine tastings are available at Rimessa Roscioli, where professional sommeliers lead you through a variety of Italian wines while outlining their qualities and provenance.

The fashionable wine bar Litro, which is situated in the Testaccio district, is well-known for its variety of organic and biodynamic wines. Small producers and lesser-known Italian wines are highlighted on the menu. In a buzzy, modern environment, it's a terrific location to find unusual and fascinating wines.

Roman wines are the focus of the Enoteca Provincia Romana, a wine store and tasting facility in the Lazio area where Rome is situated. A selection of regional wines, including those produced from lesser-known indigenous grape varietals, are available for tasting and purchase.

These wine bars and enoteche in Rome provide a broad and intriguing choice of Italian wines

2222222222

to explore and appreciate, whether you're a wine enthusiast or just like a glass of vino. Cheers!

Farmer's Market and Food Tours

You can immerse yourself in Rome's gastronomic scene and experience the city's lively food culture by visiting farmers' markets and going on food excursions. The following are various farmers' markets and culinary excursions to take into account:

Markets for produce:

Mercato di Campagna Amica del Circo Massimo: This farmers' market, which is close to the Circus Maximus, provides a variety of fresh vegetables, regional cheeses, meats, and artisanal goods. It's a fantastic location for meeting local farmers and shopping for premium foods.

Mercato di Testaccio: This lively market is located in the Testaccio area and offers a wide selection of vendors providing fresh baked products, fruits, vegetables, meats, and cheeses. It's a popular hangout for both residents and tourists because of its genuine vibe and wide range of goods.

One of Rome's biggest indoor marketplaces is Mercato Trionfale, which is close to the Vatican. A wide variety of fresh fruits, vegetables, meats, fish, spices, and other foods are available here. It's a great location for discovering Italian cuisine and purchasing regional products.

Food tours

Food excursions in Rome are available from Eating Italy Food excursions, including the well-liked "Trastevere Twilight" trip. These trips take you around the city's districts where you may sample classic Roman foods, visit nearby restaurants, and learn about the history and culture of Roman cuisine. The interpreters on these tours are informed.

The Roman Guy: The Roman Guy provides a number of food tours in Rome, such as the "Pasta-Making Class and Market Tour" and the "Rome Food and Wine Tour," which give visitors the opportunity to sample traditional

Roman cuisine, visit neighborhood markets, and discover the city's culinary customs.

Walks of Italy: Walks of Italy provides a selection of food and wine tours in Rome, such as the "Rome Food Tour: Trastevere District" and the "Wine and Food Stroll in Rome's Jewish Ghetto." These tours combine sightseeing with food tastings, allowing you to see the city's neighborhoods while indulging in delectable treats.

Eating Europe: Eating Europe provides the "Rome Twilight Trastevere Food Tour," where guests may sample authentic Roman street food, gelato, and other regional delicacies while learning about Trastevere's tastes. Their skilled tour guides provide information on Roman food and the gastronomic history of the area.

Food tours and farmers' markets are fantastic places to sample genuine Italian food, mingle with the populace, and discover the ingredients and culinary customs of Rome. They give a great culinary experience and a better grasp of the city's cuisine culture.

Cooking Classes and Culinary Experience

Cooking lessons and other culinary activities may be a great opportunity to master new skills and get first-hand experience with Italian food if you're interested in learning more about Rome's culinary traditions. Here are some choices for culinary adventures and cooking lessons in Rome:

Cookly: Cookly provides a range of cooking lessons in Rome where you can pick the brains of seasoned chefs and learn how to make classic Italian cuisine. You may choose the activity that best matches your interests and delight in crafting traditional Italian dishes from pasta-making workshops to pizza-making lessons and gelato-making sessions.

Cooking courses are available at Walks of Italy in addition to their culinary excursions, where you can learn to prepare Roman delicacies in a welcoming and comfortable setting. These lessons provide a thorough grasp of Italian culinary methods, from handmade pasta and sauces to traditional Roman cuisine.

For both amateurs and aspiring cooks, Chef Academy Rome provides long-term professional culinary programs and shorter cooking seminars. Learn how to make a variety of Italian foods, experiment with different cooking methods, and acquire understanding of the complex tastes and long culinary traditions of Italy.

Casa Mia Cooking Classes: In the center of Rome, Casa Mia Cooking Classes offers fully immersive culinary experiences. You may learn to prepare classic meals like handmade pasta, risotto, and tiramisu under the direction of knowledgeable chefs. The lessons often include going to a nearby market to choose fresh food.

Cooking Classes in a Local house: Attend a cooking class led by a Roman family and experience the friendliness and hospitality of a neighborhood house. These small-group workshops provide you the opportunity to discover true family recipes and converse about local cuisine, culture, and daily life.

Trionfale Food Market Tour and Cooking Class: This one-of-a-kind activity combines a cooking lesson with a guided tour of the Mercato Trionfale, one of Rome's biggest marketplaces. In a professional kitchen, you'll cook a delectable dinner while being guided by a chef after learning about the ingredients used in Roman cuisine and choosing fresh vegetables.

Cooking classes and other culinary experiences in Rome give you the chance to discover for yourself the methods, tastes, and customs that make Italian food so unique. You may learn new talents to dazzle family and friends while also deepening your respect for the regional culinary tradition.

DAY TRIPS AND EXCURSIONS

Tivoli: Villa d'Este and Hadrian's Villa

Villa d'Este and Hadrian's Villa are two renowned UNESCO World Heritage Sites in Tivoli, a lovely village outside of Rome. For fans of history and architecture, these historic places are must-see locations. What you need know about each of them is as follows:

Villa d'Este: Known for its lavish fountains and lovely grounds, Villa d'Este is a spectacular Renaissance mansion. The villa, which was constructed in the 16th century for Cardinal Ippolito II d'Este, is a magnificent example of Italian Renaissance architecture. The following highlights:

Those Gardens The centerpiece of Villa d'Este are the gardens, which include terraces, walkways, and a large number of fountains and other water features. Among the most well-known and artistically stunning are the Hundred Fountains, the Fountain of Neptune, and the Fountain of the Organ.

The Villa: Although the gardens are the main attraction, the villa itself is interesting to explore. Admire the exquisitely designed rooms that include frescoes, elaborate ceilings, and antique furniture. Particularly noteworthy are the Hall of the Fountain and the apartments of Cardinal Ippolito II d'Este.

Hadrian's Villa is a vast archaeological complex that was once the opulent retreat of the Roman Emperor Hadrian. It is sometimes referred to as Villa Adriana. It provides an amazing window into the emperor's life and displays the splendor and magnificence of Roman architecture. This is what you may anticipate seeing:

Emperor's Palace: The Imperial Palace, which consists of a number of structures and buildings, is the focal point of the estate. Discover the spectacular Piazza d'Oro (Golden Square), a beautifully constructed courtyard with marble and statues, and the Canopus, a sizable lake encircled by columns and sculptures.

The Maritime Theater, an artificial island encircled by a moat, is one of the attractions of Hadrian's Villa. The theater is a modest circular structure that was probably used for entertainment and private performances.

The remnants of the Greek and Latin Libraries, which once housed vast amounts of information and culture, may be found. The remnants, although being mostly ruined, provide an impression of the period's intellectual depth.

You may take in the magnificence of Renaissance and Roman buildings, explore lovely gardens, and learn about the lifestyles of the affluent and powerful in ancient times by visiting both Villa d'Este and Hadrian's Villa at Tivoli. Do not pass up the chance to see these wonderful locations around Rome that will transport you back in time.

Ostia Ancient

The archaeological site of Ostia Antica is situated about 30 kilometers southwest of Rome, close to the contemporary town of Ostia. Ostia Antica, formerly the prosperous port city of ancient Rome, provides an intriguing look into everyday life and city design in a vibrant Roman metropolis. What to anticipate while visiting Ostia Antica is as follows:

The Original Layout of the City is Displayed in the Well-Preserved Ruins of Ostia Antica. You may wander around the historic streets, see the government buildings, and envision the thriving commerce that once flourished here.

The Forum: The Forum of Ostia Antica, which included temples, basilicas, and public squares, served as the city's center. Take in the remnants of the Capitolium, which served as both the Capitoline Triad's primary temple and the hub for several minor temples.

Houses and Apartments: Explore Ostia Antica's well-preserved domestic structures to get an insight into the everyday life of the ancient Romans. Visit the House of Diana, which has stunning frescoes, and the House of the Painted Vaults, which features elaborate painted furnishings.

The Baths: Ostia Antica is home to a number of well-preserved bath facilities. The Romans cherished their communal bathing routines. The Terme di Nettuno (Baths of Neptune), which include stunning mosaics and a sizable pool, should not be missed.

At Ostia Antica, you may see a theater and an amphitheater, much as in ancient Rome. The amphitheater, where gladiatorial fights and other spectacles were held, and the theater, which can accommodate around 3,000 people each, provide insights into Roman culture and leisure time.

The Mosaics: The magnificent mosaics that decorated the floors and walls of the whole city of Ostia Antica are known throughout the world. Admire the mosaics' beautiful patterns and vivid colors as they portray legendary animals, geometric patterns, and everyday settings.

Visit the on-site museum to see the exhibits and a collection of relics that were found there. The museum gives further background and details on the importance and history of Ostia Antica.

A rare chance to go back in time and see the well-preserved ruins of a former Roman city is provided by exploring Ostia Antica. This archaeological site offers priceless insights into the everyday life, architecture, and culture of ancient Rome—from the imposing public structures to the private dwellings.

Lake Bracciano

About 32 kilometers northwest of Rome, in the Italian province of Lazio, lies the charming lake known as Lake Bracciano. Lake Bracciano provides a calm retreat from the busy metropolis since it is surrounded by undulating hills and attractive historic villages. What to expect while visiting Lake Bracciano is as follows:

Enjoy the natural splendor of Lake Bracciano's surroundings. An idyllic and tranquil atmosphere is created by the lake's crystal-clear waters, abundant flora, and calm scenery. Enjoy leisurely strolls along the coastline or just sit back and take it all in.

Lake Bracciano is a great place to go for water sports and recreational activities. You may take your time exploring the lake by renting kayaks, paddleboards, or small boats. Another well-liked activity is sailing and windsurfing, and there are several sailing schools and rental businesses available.

Visit the quaint village of Bracciano, which is situated on the lake's southern side. Discover the historic center's winding lanes made of cobblestones, its medieval structures, and its quaint piazzas. Avoid missing the majestic Renaissance fortress Castello Orsini-Odescalchi, which towers above the town and the lake.

Anguillara Sabazia: Anguillara Sabazia is yet another lovely village on the banks of Lake

Bracciano. This delightful medieval town has lovely lake views, a quaint old center, and a promenade where you can take a leisurely walk. Visit one of the lakeside cafés or restaurants to indulge in regional cuisine while taking in the beautiful scenery.

Trevignano Romano is a charming village with winding lanes, brightly painted homes, and a bustling lakefront promenade. It is situated on the western coast of the lake. Visit the Church of Santa Maria Assunta, stroll around the town's historic district, and stand on the shore to take in the expansive views of the lake.

Nature Reserves: The nature reserves that border Lake Bracciano provide chances for hiking, birding, and discovering the regional flora and fauna. Both the neighboring Canale Monterano Nature Reserve and the Martignano Nature Reserve provide peaceful environments for outdoor enthusiasts.

Enjoy the regional cuisine when visiting the Lake Bracciano region. Freshwater fish from the lake are well-known, especially the famed "coregone" (lake whitefish). Enjoy a leisurely supper at one of the lakeside eateries while indulging in handmade pasta, fresh fish dishes, and other regional favorites.

An idyllic and attractive getaway from the busy metropolis of Rome is provided by Lake Bracciano. This stunning lake and the cities that surround it have something to offer any tourist, whether they're looking for leisure, outdoor recreation, or cultural discovery.

Castelli Romani

A beautiful location known as the Castelli Romani, or "Roman Castles," is situated in the hills southeast of Rome, Italy. The Castelli Romani area, well-known for its charming villages, breathtaking vistas, and vineyards, provides a lovely escape from the city. The following are some of the region's highlights:

One of the most well-known towns in the Castelli Romani is Frascati. This picturesque town, known for producing white wine, has gorgeous vistas, old houses, and a lovely historic center. Explore the Piazza del Gesù, the city's central plaza surrounded by cafés and restaurants, and pay a visit to the majestic

Renaissance Villa Aldobrandini with its lovely gardens.

Castel Gandolfo is well known as the Pope's vacation retreat and is perched atop a hill overlooking Lake Albano. The Apostolic residence of Castel Gandolfo, a papal residence in the city, is accessible to the public for visits. Take in the expansive vistas of Lake Albano while exploring the old district's winding streets.

Nemi: This lakeside community is well-known for its wild strawberries and its connections to early Roman culture. Discover the remnants of two historic Roman ships that formerly sailed on Lake Nemi at the Museo delle Navi Romane (Museum of Roman Ships). Discover the town's quaint streets, indulge in regional specialties, and enjoy the stunning lake vistas.

Rocca di Papa: Rocca di Papa, which is located at the highest point of the Castelli Romani, provides breathtaking panoramic views of the surroundings. Enjoy the local food at one of the town's restaurants after taking a leisurely walk through the streets and stopping at the Church of the Assumption.

Lake Albano: Lake Albano and Lake Nemi are two lovely lakes located in the Castelli Romani region. The larger of the two lakes, Lake Albano, provides chances for outdoor pursuits including swimming, kayaking, and boating. Enjoy a picnic while appreciating the serene surroundings, join a boat excursion, or just unwind on the lakeside beaches.

Wine tasting: The Castelli Romani area is well known for its long history of winemaking. Visit nearby vineyards and wineries as part of a wine tour to taste some of the area's well-known red wines, such as Frascati, Marino, and Castelli Romani. Discover the process of creating wine, take a tour through the vineyards, and savor the tastes of the regional wines.

A great location for visitors seeking a blend of history, scenic beauty, and gastronomic pleasures is the Castelli Romani area. With its quaint villages, breathtaking scenery, and rich cultural legacy, this region makes for the ideal getaway from the city and a chance to see the real Italian countryside.

Mount Vesuvius and Pompeii

In the vicinity of Naples, Italy, are two well-known locations noted for its historical importance and natural beauty: Pompeii and Mount Vesuvius. What you should know before visiting these wonderful sights is as follows:

Pompeii: Following Mount Vesuvius' disastrous eruption in 79 AD, the ancient Roman city of Pompeii was submerged under several feet of volcanic ash and pumice. It is now a remarkable archaeological site that offers a rare look into everyday life in a Roman city in antiquity. Important sights include:
The Ruins: Take a tour of the impressively well-preserved Pompeiian ruins, which include homes, shops, temples, and civic structures. The Forum, the Amphitheater, the House of the Faun, and the Villa of the Mysteries, which is renowned for its magnificent paintings, are just a few of the highlights.

The Pompeii Archaeological Museum is a local attraction where you may see the mosaics, sculptures, and daily items that have been found from Pompeii. More details about the customs and culture of the old city are revealed by the museum.

The fabled volcano known as Mount Vesuvius famously erupted in 79 AD, burying Pompeii and Herculaneum. It is now one of the most well-known and active volcanoes in the planet. What to anticipate while visiting Mount Vesuvius is as follows:
Hiking to the Crater: Join a guided excursion to ascend to Mount Vesuvius' crater. As you climb the mountain, take in the expansive views of the surroundings. When you reach the crater, you can see for yourself how the location was molded by nature's strong forces.

Visit the Volcanic Observatory and Information Center, which is situated close to the entrance, before going on a hike. Through educational displays and exhibits, find out more about the geology, history, and present activity of the volcano.

Safety precautions: It is crucial to abide by the safety instructions given by the authorities since Mount Vesuvius is a volcanic mountain. Carry water, wear suitable footwear, pay attention to the weather, and take note of any warnings about upcoming volcanic activity.

Suggestions for visiting Mount Vesuvius and Pompeii:

Plan your trip: From Naples, you may go alone to Pompeii or Mount Vesuvius, or you can join a tour group. Make sure to account for this in your schedule and allow enough time to visit each location.

Consider taking a trip that is led through Pompeii and Mount Vesuvius. A competent guide can enrich your experience by sharing insights about the sites' geological importance, history, and culture.

comfy clothes: As you will be walking and trekking quite a bit, wear comfy shoes and clothes. Be ready for any weather, particularly if you want to hike Mount Vesuvius.

Exploring Roman history and taking in the majestic force of a volcanic setting are both made possible by visiting Pompeii and Mount Vesuvius. These locations are bound to make an impact, whether you're entranced by the archaeological remains of Pompeii or fascinated by the geological marvels of Mount Vesuvius.

Orvieto

The picturesque hilltop town of Orvieto is situated in central Italy's Umbria region. Orvieto is a place that tourists really must visit because of its extensive history, gorgeous architecture, and panoramic vistas. What to anticipate while visiting Orvieto is as follows:

Orvieto's beautiful Duomo, one of Italy's most stunning churches, serves as the town's focal point. Admire its magnificent Gothic façade, which is embellished with deft carvings and vibrant mosaics. Step inside to see the chapel of San Brizio, which has stunning murals by Luca Signorelli, and the opulent interior.

Explore the subterranean tunnels, caverns, and historic wells of Orvieto by going below the city's streets. The interesting network of tunnels cut into the tuff rock and the city's Etruscan roots are both shown during guided tours of the Orvieto Underground.

St. Patrick's Well, a spectacular technical achievement from the 16th century, may be found in Pozzo di San Patrizio. Visitors may reach the water source at the foot of this double-helix stairway while also enjoying a distinctive architectural experience.

Historic core of Orvieto: Stroll through the lovely squares and winding lanes of Orvieto's historic core. Everywhere you look, take in the stunning scenery, charming boutiques, and historic buildings. The town hall and a small museum are located in the stunning medieval Palazzo del Popolo.

Discover the artistic and cultural heritage of Orvieto by visiting the town's museums and art galleries. The National Archaeological Museum showcases Etruscan relics, while the Orvieto subterranean Museum offers insights into the city's subterranean past. Don't overlook the Museo Claudio Faina, which has a collection of antique ceramics and antiquities from the Etruscan period.

Enjoy the regional food and wine of Orvieto, which is renowned for its delectable dishes and top-notch wines. Try the local white wine Orvieto Classico and try some of the local specialties including porchetta (roast pig), wild boar, and truffles from Umbria. To experience the genuine tastes of the area, explore the neighborhood wine bars and trattorias.

Panoramic vistas: From Orvieto's high points, take in breath-taking vistas of the surrounding landscape. The town's location on a plateau of volcanic rock affords breathtaking views of the surrounding hills, vineyards, and villages in the distance. For a comprehensive perspective of the town and its surroundings, climb the medieval tower known as the Torre del Moro.

Orvieto is a fascinating location in central Italy because of its beauty, history, and gastronomic treats. Orvieto is certain to create a lasting impression, whether you're discovering its mysterious subterranean caverns, awe-struck by its magnificent architecture, or indulging in its regional cuisine.

Florence:A Day Trip to the City of the Renaissance

The cradle of the Renaissance, Florence, is a veritable treasure mine of artistic, historical, and architectural marvels. Even if one day is insufficient to thoroughly see Florence, it is still possible to have an enjoyable day trip and take in the attractions of the city. A proposed route for a day excursion to Florence is shown below:

Beginning with the Duomo Start your day at Florence's Piazza del Duomo, the city's central square. Admire the gorgeous dome Brunelleschi created for the famous Florence Cathedral, popularly known as the Duomo. Enjoy the cathedral's ornate exterior and go to the dome's summit for sweeping views of the city.

Visit the Uffizi Gallery: Visit the adjacent Uffizi Gallery, one of the most recognized art galleries in the world. Admire the works of art created by famous artists including Botticelli, Michelangelo, Raphael, and Leonardo da Vinci. To save time and avoid lengthy lines, purchase your tickets in advance.

Visit the Accademia Gallery: Head over to the Accademia Gallery, which is home to Michelangelo's David, one of the most well-known statues in the whole world. Explore the various pieces of art on show while admiring the fine intricacies of this renowned masterpiece.

Ponte Vecchio and the Arno River: Pass across the charming Ponte Vecchio, a medieval bridge surrounded by boutiques offering jewelry, trinkets, and regional crafts. Take in the magnificent views of the city and its bridges as you slowly walk along the Arno River.

Piazza della Signoria: Make your way to this famous plaza, known for its amazing statues and old structures. Take some time to see the replica of Michelangelo's David and the outdoor sculpture museum in front of the Palazzo Vecchio.

Enjoy some authentic Florentine cuisine by treating yourself to a supper at one of the city's famed trattorias. Try regional favorites like ribollita (Tuscan soup), gelato for dessert, and bistecca alla fiorentina (Florentine steak).

Cross the Ponte Santa Trinita to enter the area noted for its artisan workshops and genuine charm, the Oltrarno neighborhood, and explore it. Visit the Pitti Palace and its lovely Boboli Gardens for a tranquil walk among verdant foliage and magnificent statues.

Before departing Florence, go to the Piazzale Michelangelo, a panoramic area that provides breath-taking views of the city. Enjoy the sunset there. When the sun is setting, arrive to see the city's skyline drenched in golden tones.

In order to get the most of your time in Florence, remember to pack comfortable shoes and organize your day well. Florence has so much more to offer than what this schedule can ever cover, so think about coming back for a longer stay in the future.

SHOPPING AND FASHION

Luxury Shopping Areas

If you're looking for a high-end shopping experience, Florence has a number of upmarket shopping areas with renowned fashion shops, designer brands, and posh stores. Here are a few of Florence's premier areas for luxury shopping:

High-end fashion companies and well-known worldwide brands line the Via de' Tornabuoni, which is regarded as Florence's most elegant and opulent shopping strip. The likes of Gucci, Prada, Salvatore Ferragamo, Bulgari, and others may be found here. Spend some time perusing the chic stores and marveling at the exquisite window displays.

Via della Vigna Nuova is a parallel to Via de' Tornabuoni premium retail route that has a curated collection of luxury products. This boulevard is a fashion lover's dream, with worldwide brands like Hermès and Chanel mixing with Italian designers like Roberto Cavalli and Emilio Pucci.

In addition to serving as Florence's main plaza, Piazza della Repubblica is also a bustling commercial district. Luxury department shops, such as Rinascente and LuisaViaRoma, which are renowned for their upscale collections of clothing, accessories, and cosmetics, can be found all around the plaza.

Via dei Calzaiuoli: This busy route, which links Piazza del Duomo and Piazza della Signoria, is lined with a mix of high-end and mass-market goods. Discover luxury retailers like Max Mara, Longchamp, and Church's as well as well-known global brands like Zara and H&M.

The Mall is an upscale outlet shopping destination situated near Leccio, around 30 minutes outside of Florence, if you're prepared to go a little bit outside of the city. Prestigious labels like Gucci, Prada, Armani, and Dolce & Gabbana are represented at this upmarket outlet complex, giving lower pricing on their high-end goods.

Salvatore Ferragamo Museum and Boutique: A visit to the Salvatore Ferragamo Museum and Boutique is essential for fashion fans interested in the development of Italian luxury. The museum, which is housed in Palazzo Spini Feroni, features the famed Italian shoe designer Ferragamo's classic creations. Discover the historical exhibitions about the company, and then peruse the newest designs in the store next door.

Keep in mind that opening hours may vary and that certain shops may need appointments for specialized shopping experiences as you explore these upscale shopping areas. Be ready to pay more as well since luxury things sometimes have greater expenses. Nevertheless, for fashion connoisseurs and those looking for upmarket retail therapy, going on a luxury shopping spree in Florence may be a lovely experience.

Markets On The Street And Flea Markets

Aside from the high-end luxury stores, Florence provides a wide range of street markets and flea markets where you may find one-of-a-kind things, regional goods, and antique treasures. Here are a few of Florence's well-liked street markets and flea markets:

Mercato di San Lorenzo is one of Florence's biggest and most well-known marketplaces, and it is situated close to the Basilica of San Lorenzo. The leather products sold at this crowded indoor market, such as purses, jackets, belts, and other items, are well-known. Additionally, there are kiosks offering local foods, accessories, apparel, and souvenirs. Negotiating pricing is customary here, so don't be afraid to do so.

Mercato di Sant'Ambrogio is a bustling neighborhood market where you may experience Florentine everyday life. It is tucked away in the Sant'Ambrogio area. A vast variety of fresh products, including fruits, vegetables, dairy, meats, and seafood, are available at this outdoor market. If you have access to a kitchen, it's a terrific location to enjoy the regional cuisine and shop for ingredients.

The major flea market in Florence is called Mercato delle Pulci, and it is situated at Piazza dei Ciompi. This market, which is open every day, is a veritable gold mine of furniture, books, collectibles, antiques, and vintage goods. Look among the booths to see if you can locate one-of-a-kind items to bring home as mementos or to decorate your house with a little history.

Mercato Nuovo, sometimes referred to as the Straw Market, is a covered arcade that is close to the Ponte Vecchio. The market sells a variety of leather items, scarves, trinkets, and regional commodities like olive oil and honey, however it is most known for the well-known bronze statue of a wild boar (Il Porcellino), which people massage for good luck.

Piazza Santo Spirito's Fiera Antiquaria: Every second Sunday of the month, Piazza Santo Spirito plays home to a bustling antique market. You may look through a variety of old furniture, clothes from bygone eras, jewelry, pottery, books, and other items here. It's a well-liked destination for antique enthusiasts and collectors, providing a chance to discover rare and historic items.

The Mercatino dell'Artigianato is an artisan market that features the creations of regional craftspeople. It is held at Piazza Santa Croce on certain weekends throughout the year. Browse through handcrafted crafts such as leather goods, textiles, leather jewelry, and ceramics. It's a wonderful chance to buy handcrafted, one-of-a-kind things and support regional craftsmen.

It's a good idea to call ahead to confirm the opening days and hours before visiting these markets since they may change. Be ready to negotiate crowds as well, especially during the busiest travel seasons. Discovering hidden treasures, interacting with local merchants, and locating one-of-a-kind souvenirs of your vacation may all be had by exploring Florence's street markets and flea markets.

Fashion Outlets and Designer Brands

There are a few places that provide a large range of luxury and high-end fashion at more moderate costs if you're seeking for designer brands at reduced pricing or fashion outlet shopping close to Florence. Here are some well-known fashion stores and locations for designer brands close to Florence:

The Mall Luxury Outlet is a prime location for luxury outlet shopping and is situated in Leccio, approximately 30 minutes from Florence. Numerous renowned fashion houses are represented, including Gucci, Prada, Armani, Dolce & Gabbana, Valentino, and others. Discounts are available at the Mall on a range of items including apparel, footwear, accessories, and even home furnishings. It offers an opulent outlet shopping experience with its magnificent location and stunning Tuscan background.

Barberino Designer Outlet: The Barberino Designer Outlet is a well-liked shopping location and is located in Barberino di Mugello, approximately 30 kilometers from Florence. Designer names including Michael Kors, Hugo Boss, Polo Ralph Lauren, Versace, and others are included. Discounts are available at the store on clothing, accessories, athletics, and home goods.

Prada Space: The Prada Space is an exclusive outlet shop for the famous Italian brand Prada and is situated in Montevarchi, around 45 kilometers from Florence. Past-season products from Prada and Miu Miu, a sibling company, are on sale here. A variety of apparel, purses, shoes, and accessories are available at the shop.

Fashion Valley is a retail center with various designer stores that is located near Reggello, some 40 kilometers southeast of Florence. It includes names like Hogan, Roberto Cavalli, Ermanno Scervino, and others. At bargain rates, you may get a selection of stylish accessories, shoes, and clothes.

Designer Outlet Valdichiana: The Designer Outlet Valdichiana is a sizable retail complex featuring a variety of designer brands. It is situated close to Arezzo, around 80 kilometers southeast of Florence. It provides cheap fashion products from labels like Versace, Gucci, Prada, Fendi, and more.

Designer brands may be purchased at these outlets at lower costs than they would in their usual retail locations. It's important to keep in mind that the availability of certain brands and discounts may change, so it's best to check the websites of the retailers or get in touch with them directly for the most recent information. Additionally, to get to these businesses from Florence comfortably, think about your transportation alternatives, such hiring a vehicle or using shuttle services.

Craftsmanship and Artisan Shops

Florence is recognized for its long history of artisanal skill and workmanship. Numerous artisan stores can be found around the city where you can browse one-of-a-kind, handmade goods and see experienced artisans at work. Here are some Florence craft stores and businesses to visit:

Leather Products: Florence is well known for its leather workmanship. To discover excellent leather goods including purses, wallets, belts, coats, and shoes, visit artisan leather stores in the city, especially those around the San Lorenzo Market and the Santa Croce neighborhood. Look for stores that have an emphasis on traditional methods and premium materials.

Florence is renowned for its historical paper manufacturing and bookbinding culture. Explore a variety of gorgeous handmade stationery, notebooks, diaries, and ornamental papers by visiting artisan paper stores like Il Papiro and Giulio Giannini e Figlio. Additionally, you may locate bookbinding-specific businesses where you can see how books are made and repaired by hand.

Pottery & ceramics: Florence has a long history of producing fine ceramics. Find artisan pottery stores where you can get handcrafted ceramics, beautiful pottery, and ornamental goods in locales including the Oltrarno district and Santo Spirito neighborhood. Look for stores that feature old-fashioned methods like hand painting and glazing.

Florence is a center for the creation of magnificent jewelry. Investigate artisan jewelry stores that sell one-of-a-kind, exquisitely handmade items made using age-old methods.

139)

Find one-of-a-kind jewelry pieces that honor the city's creative legacy by visiting jewelers that specialize in goldsmithing, gemstone setting, and filigree work.

Woodworking and marquetry: The practice of inlaying wood with complex motifs has a long history in Florence. Look for artisan workshops where you may see talented woodworkers constructing lovely wooden products, furniture, and ornamental items utilizing customary woodworking methods.

Experience the unique art of Florentine paper marbling, sometimes referred to as "memorizzazione." Visit artisan studios or workshops to see how brilliant colors and swirling patterns are used to create one-of-a-kind marbled paper masterpieces. These lovely materials are used for creative projects, stationery, and book covers.

Florence is recognized for its skill in the restoration of works of art. Investigate the restoration and conservation of paintings, sculptures, and other creative creations in workshops and studios. There are several locations that provide guided tours where you may discover the delicate procedures needed to preserve and restore precious artworks.

These are just a few examples of the handiwork and artisan stores Florence has to offer. Numerous additional studios and stores devoted to preserving traditional crafts and supporting regional craftsmen are likely to be found as you tour the city. Spend some time conversing with the artisans, learning about their methods, and appreciating the talent and love they put into their work.

Vintage and Secondhand Stores

If you like vintage apparel, Florence has a wide selection of vintage and used shops where you may find one-of-a-kind and distinctive clothing, accessories, and other treasures. The following Florence vintage and used shops are noteworthy:

Epoca: A well-known vintage store with a carefully chosen variety of vintage clothes and accessories for both men and women, Epoca is situated close to Piazza Santa Croce. The shop sells a variety of designer brands and one-of-a-kind treasures together with high-quality vintage items from various periods.

Desii Vintage is a lovely store with a wide selection of vintage apparel, accessories, and jewelry that is located in the Oltrarno district of Buenos Aires. You may discover a variety of vintage things that represent many styles and eras, from exquisite gowns to retro accessories.

Recollection Vintage is a well-known vintage shop that sells a variety of well chosen apparel and accessories from different periods. It is located in the Santa Maria Novella neighborhood. Vintage dresses, jackets, purses, and scarves are all available, making them ideal for anybody looking for one-of-a-kind clothing items with a historical flair.

Cenci Vintage is a well-known vintage and used shop with a large assortment of apparel, accessories, and jewelry that is close to Piazza della Repubblica. The shop offers products from well-known designer names as well as lesser-known labels, offering a varied choice of vintage treasures. It serves both men and women.

A treasure trove of antique apparel, accessories, and home décor can be found at Fania antique, a store in the San Frediano district. The shop sells a variety of vintage items that have been meticulously chosen, such as dresses, coats, hats, and distinctive accessories that encapsulate previous design trends.

Mercato di Antiquariato (Antiques Market): The Antiques Market is a collection of exhibitors offering vintage and antique goods such furniture, clothes, jewelry, and antiques. It is held on the third Sunday of every month in Florence's old center. It's a wonderful chance to discover a variety of antique discoveries in a romantic outdoor environment.

Keep in mind that each of these vintage and secondhand shops has its own distinct selection and price guidelines when you visit. Before going, it's usually a good idea to verify the store's opening and closing times. Additionally, have a good eye for finding hidden jewels amid the racks and be willing to devote some time. It might be fun to go vintage shopping in Florence, where you can indulge in the nostalgia of bygone times and give your clothing a vintage flare.

Souvenirs and Local Product

You may purchase a variety of trinkets and regional goods that are a reflection of Florence's rich cultural past while visiting the city. Here are some well-liked mementos and regional goods to take into consideration, whether you're looking for traditional crafts, specialty foods and wines, or one-of-a-kind keepsakes:

Leather products: Florence is well-known for its expert leathercraft. Look for leather accessories like purses, wallets, belts, and jackets, which come in a variety of designs and hues. To locate genuine, handmade leather goods, go to artisan leather stores and marketplaces, such the San Lorenzo Market or the Santa Croce neighborhood.

Florentine Paper: Making paper has a long history in Florence. Bring home stationery, notebooks, diaries, or decorative papers with exquisite designs crafted using age-old methods. To see a large variety of Florentine paper goods, go to specialty paper stores like Il Papiro or Giulio Giannini e Figlio.

Jewelry crafted by hand: Florence is renowned for its excellent jewelry design. Look for handcrafted jewelry with elaborate patterns and excellent craftsmanship that is produced from precious metals and gemstones. Discover one-of-a-kind, handmade jewelry at stores and studios that showcase Florentine craftsmanship.

Florence has a long history of producing fine ceramics and pottery. Think about investing in hand-painted dinnerware, colorful tiles, or pottery with classic patterns and brilliant hues. Look in neighborhoods like the Oltrarno district or the Santo Spirito neighborhood for stores that specialize in ceramics.

Reproductions of Florentine Art: Florence is home to some of the finest works of art in history. Replicas of well-known works of art, such as Michelangelo's "David" and Botticelli's "The Birth of Venus," are available. To locate prints, postcards, or even miniature versions of famous sculptures, search respected art galleries or museum gift stores.

145)

Local Cuisine and Wine: Florence is well known for its delectable cuisine. Bring some local produce and culinary delights with you. Purchase some extra virgin olive oil, balsamic vinegar, Chianti wine, or truffle items. To discover classic Tuscan goods like Pecorino cheese, salami, or handcrafted pasta, you may also browse neighborhood food markets.

Products Made from Florentine Marbled Paper: "Marmorizzazione," or marbled paper, is a specialty of Florence. Look for paper goods with this unique design on bookmarks, journals, or other items. Items made on marbled paper are lovely and distinctive keepsakes that highlight the city's creative past.

High-quality cosmetics and fragrances have been produced in Florence for a very long time. Discover locally produced scents, soaps, and skincare items that showcase the elegance and workmanship of the city by visiting perfume stores or cosmetic boutiques.

Consider supporting regional craftsmen and small companies while buying trinkets and regional goods in Florence. Find stores that place an emphasis on sustainable business methods and traditional workmanship. You

146)

will have a wide variety of alternatives when you explore the city's marketplaces, stores, and workshops, enabling you to locate special souvenirs that encapsulate Florence's distinctive culture and tradition.

Tips for Shopping and Bargaining

Here are some helpful pointers and advice for navigating the local retail scene and improving your experience when shopping in Florence:

Study and Planning: Before starting your shopping spree, do some study to get acquainted with Florence's well-known shopping districts, marketplaces, and shops. Make a list of the precise products you're thinking about getting to help you focus your search.

Timing: Be aware that many businesses in Florence take "la pausa," or a midday break, often between 1:00 PM and 3:30 PM. To prevent disappointment and to guarantee that the shops you wish to visit are open, plan your shopping properly.

Italian workmanship is renowned for its excellent quality and authenticity. Be mindful of the materials, finishes, and workmanship when buying things like leather goods, jewelry, or artwork. Look for authenticity seals or proof that the product was manufactured locally or by hand.

Bargaining: In the majority of Florence's retail stores, haggling is uncommon. In open-air marketplaces, however, especially while buying apparel, accessories, or souvenirs, it could be more acceptable. If you believe there is an opportunity for bargaining, use your judgment and bargain respectfully, but keep in mind to respect the seller's privacy.

VAT Refund: Non-EU citizens who make qualified purchases may be entitled to a VAT (Value Added Tax) refund. Find stores that provide tax-free shopping and request the relevant documentation. Before leaving Italy, claim your VAT refund at the airport or other approved refund locations by keeping your receipts and following the refund procedure.

Local Markets: There are a number of lively markets in Florence, including the San Lorenzo Market, where you can buy a broad range of products, including clothes, leather goods, souvenirs, and more. Remember that market pricing is often adjustable, so if you're interested in anything, feel free to participate in some cordial haggling.

The majority of Florence's stores open at approximately 9:30 AM and shut at between 7:30 PM and 8:00 PM. However, these times may change, particularly on holidays or in more intimate boutique stores. Plan appropriately, giving yourself plenty of time to browse without feeling pressured.

Payment Options: The majority of Florence's stores and shops take major credit cards, but it's always a good idea to have some cash on hand in case you encounter any smaller businesses, markets, or street sellers that may only accept cash payments. If you need to make a cash withdrawal, ATMs are conveniently located around the city.

Customs and shipment: If you want to buy expensive or delicate things, find out the store's delivery policies. Frequently, they might set up shipping services to your own nation. To guarantee a simple procedure for any commodities subject to customs charges or

149)

limitations, familiarize yourself with the customs laws of your native nation.

Don't forget to take in the distinctive ambiance, mingle with the local artists, and enjoy your shopping experience in Florence. Shopping in this wonderful city gives you the chance to find exquisite workmanship and bring home lovely souvenirs that will make you think of your stay in Florence.

PRACTICAL INFORMATION

Rome's Transportation

To make it easier for you to get about Rome, there are a number of transit choices available. Here are a few of the typical transit options in Rome:

Rome features a comprehensive metro system that connects the city's many neighborhoods. Three lines make up the Metro: Line A in red, Line B in blue, and Line C in green. It's a quick and effective method to get to Rome's many districts and top attractions.

Bus: Rome has a robust bus system that connects the whole city, including important tourist attractions. Buses are a practical form of transportation, particularly in locations where the metro does not operate. Buses operated by ATAC may be found all throughout the city.

Rome has a network of tram lines that function in conjunction with the metro and bus systems. Trams are very helpful for getting to communities and places where there isn't much access to the metro. Both residents and visitors like them since they provide a picturesque form of transportation.

Taxi: Taxis are generally accessible in Rome and may be located at marked taxi stops or called on the street. Find certified taxis with proper signs, meters, and license plates. Before getting in, it's a good idea to double check the rate since taxis often charge more for things like bags or late-night trips.

Rome has a "Roma Bike" or "Biciroma" bike-sharing program that enables you to hire bicycles for short excursions within the city. In order to hire and return bikes, look for bike stations with specialized apps or kiosks.

Electric Scooters: In Rome, electric scooters from brands like Lime, Bird, or Helbiz are becoming more and more well-liked. utilizing a smartphone app, renting and utilizing these scooters is simple. Keep in mind to park them safely and abide by the regulations of the road.

Traveling on foot is the greatest way to see Rome, particularly in the old city center where numerous sites are close to one another. You can take in the ambience, find hidden jewels, and fully enjoy the old-world beauty of the city by walking.

Train: The train is a great alternative if you want to visit locations outside of Rome, such neighboring cities or villages. Rome's primary railway station, Roma Termini, provides service to both domestic and foreign locations.

It is advised to buy tickets in advance and validate them before boarding buses, trams, or entering the metro while traveling in Rome. Single trip tickets, daily or multi-day passes, or the Roma Pass, which grants unlimited access to public transit and reduced admission to selected attractions, are available as ticket alternatives.

Rome's ZTL (Limited Traffic Zones), which limit car access in certain sections of the city center, are another factor to take into account. For advice on parking and entering restricted areas, it is essential to consult your lodging provider or rental vehicle company.

Rome's transportation system offers a selection of solutions to meet your requirements and taste. Select the means of transportation that best fits your travel plans, then take pleasure in discovering the Eternal City.

Emergency and Safety Contacts

Rome is no exception; safety is always the first consideration while visiting anywhere. Here are some crucial safety advice and emergency numbers to keep in mind while there:

Be mindful of your surroundings, particularly in congested places and at tourist destinations. Be careful not to flaunt costly jewelry or big sums of cash out in the open.

To keep your possessions safe, use a money belt or a bag with a lock.

Keep your luggage closed and near your body, and be on the lookout for pickpockets.

Keep to crowded, well-lit locations, particularly at night.

Utilize legal and reliable taxis or other transit options.

Avoid dealing with street sellers that offer fake items or are involved in illicit activity.

Emergency numbers:

In case of an emergency, dial 112 or 113 to get in touch with the police.

Medical Emergency: For ambulance services and medical emergencies, dial 118.

Fire Department: To report a fire or request the fire department's aid, dial 115.

Tourist Police: The Carabinieri may be contacted at +39 06 4888 2424 or +39 06 4888 2920 for assistance with tourist-related issues.

Health and Safety: Travel insurance that pays for emergencies and medical costs is a good idea.

Take a copy of your passport with you and store the original somewhere secure.

Find out where the nearby hospitals or medical facilities are and get familiar with their location.

When eating food and liquids, use caution. Consume only bottled water and only at recognized restaurants.

Knowing the generic names of your drugs is important if you have any pre-existing medical issues or need to take a certain prescription.

Stay hydrated and use sunscreen, particularly in the summer when temperatures may soar.

Local Laws and traditions: To guarantee that you respect local culture and prevent any legal complications, familiarize yourself with the local laws and traditions of Rome.

Avoid participating in unlawful activities like buying counterfeit items or using drugs.

Keep track of any safety or travel advisories that your embassy or consulate may issue.

It's crucial to remember that these safety recommendations are just general advice, so it's best to apply care and common sense when visiting Rome. To have a safe and happy trip in the city, be educated, follow your gut, and take the appropriate steps.

Using Language and Expressions

It's beneficial to know a few basic Italian phrases and the local language before visiting

Rome. Here are some helpful words and phrases to help you when visiting Rome:

Greetings:
Hello: Ciao (chow)
Good morning: Buongiorno (bwohn-JOR-noh)
Good evening: Buonasera (bwoh-nah-SEH-rah)
Goodbye: Arrivederci (ah-ree-veh-DAIR-chee)
Polite Expressions:
Please: Per favore (pehr fa-VOH-ray)
Thank you: Grazie (GRAHTS-yeh)
You're welcome: Prego (PREH-goh)
Excuse me: Mi scusi (mee SKOO-zee)
I'm sorry: Mi dispiace (mee dees-pee-AH-che)
Basic Conversational Phrases:
Do you speak English?: Parla inglese? (PAR-lah een-GLAY-zeh?)
I don't understand: Non capisco (non kah-PEES-koh)
Can you help me?: Mi può aiutare? (mee pwoh ah-YOO-tah-ray)
Where is...?: Dove si trova...? (DOH-veh see TROH-vah)
How much does it cost?: Quanto costa? (KWAHN-toh KOH-stah)
Ordering Food and Drinks:
Menu, please: Il menu, per favore (eel MEH-noo, pehr fa-VOH-ray)

I would like...: Vorrei... (vor-RAY)
Coffee: Caffè (kah-FAY)
Water: Acqua (AHK-kwah)
Beer: Birra (BEER-rah)
Wine: Vino (VEE-noh)
Getting Around:
Where is the nearest...?: Dove si trova il più vicino...? (DOH-veh see TROH-vah eel pwee vee-CHEE-noh)
Train station: Stazione ferroviaria (sta-TSYOH-neh feh-RO-vya-ree-ah)
Metro station: Stazione della metropolitana (sta-TSYOH-neh DEHL-la meh-troh-poh-lee-TAH-nah)
Bus stop: Fermata dell'autobus (fehr-MAH-tah DEHL-lah-oo-TOH-boos)
Numbers:
One: Uno (OO-noh)
Two: Due (DOO-eh)
Three: Tre (TREH)
Ten: Dieci (DEE-eh-chee)
Twenty: Venti (VEN-tee)
Hundred: Cento (CHEN-toh)

A little effort at speaking Italian is welcomed by locals and may improve your encounters, so keep that in mind. If you need explanation or assistance, don't be afraid to ask since most Italians are amiable and willing to help.

Currency and Tipping

You may properly manage your funds during your vacation to Rome if you are aware of the local currency, payment options, and tipping practices. Here are some details on monetary issues and tips in Rome:

The Euro (€) is the official unit of exchange in Italy. In Rome, it is widely recognized, and there are several ATMs where you may get cash. Hotels, restaurants, and retail establishments all take major credit cards like Visa and Mastercard.

currency Rates: Before exchanging money, it is a good idea to verify the current currency rates. Banks and authorized exchange offices provide reasonable rates, but it is advised to compare rates and fees to make sure you are getting the best deal possible. Do not exchange money with unlicensed street sellers.

Payment Options: Cash is still a common payment method in Rome, particularly for quick purchases and in small businesses. Credit and debit cards, however, are routinely accepted, especially at bigger retailers, restaurants, and hotels. It's a good idea to have a variety of cards and cash with you to make life easier and be ready for anything.

Tipping is not as common or anticipated in Italy, notably Rome, as it is in some other nations. However, it's customary to offer a little tip as a sign of gratitude for excellent service. Here are some suggestions for standard gratuities:

In restaurants, a service fee is often included in the bill and is usually noted as "servizio incluso." If it is not, leaving a tip of 5–10% of the total cost is appreciated but not required.
Tipping is not anticipated while purchasing a short coffee or a drink at the bar. However, if you have table service and sit at a table, you may round up the price or add a little gratuity.
Taxi: As a show of gratitude, it's customary to round up the fare or give a modest tip.
Hotel Staff: Leaving a modest tip is appreciated, but not required, if hotel staff members such as the concierge or cleaning provide you with great service.
Service Fees: A coperto (cover fee) may be added to the bill at certain restaurants,

especially those that cater to tourists. Bread and table service are included at this fee. When reading your bill, be mindful of this fee.

Pricing and Receipts: Taxes and service fees are frequently included in retail and restaurant prices. Asking for a receipt (scontrino) is typical since they can be needed for warranty claims or tax refunds.

Keep in mind that Rome does not require tips, and your decision to leave one will ultimately depend on how happy you were with the service. If you're unsure whether to give a tip, use your judgment and keep in mind local customs.

It's wise to let your bank or credit card provider know about your vacation intentions to guarantee smooth card use and to find out if there will be any foreign transaction fees.

You may manage your cash smoothly and without problem when visiting Rome if you are aware of these money-related issues and the city's tipping practices.

Connectivity and the Internet

To navigate, communicate, and obtain helpful information while visiting Rome, you must maintain an internet connection. Information about internet and connection alternatives in the city is provided below:

SIM cards with mobile data:
Buying a local SIM card is an economical and practical choice if you have an unlocked smartphone. In the city's airports, railway stations, and mobile network stores, you may purchase SIM cards from a variety of carriers.
Italy's top mobile network providers, TIM, Vodafone, and WindTre, provide prepaid SIM cards with data plans for travelers. Choose a plan based on its data allotment and validity after comparing the available ones.
In order to register and activate a SIM card in Italy, don't forget to carry your passport.
Wi-Fi:
In most hotels, cafés, restaurants, and public areas in Rome, clients may use free Wi-Fi. Ask the employees for the network name and password or keep an eye out for signage suggesting Wi-Fi availability.
Additionally, a lot of public spaces and tourist destinations provide free Wi-Fi hotspots.

Popular squares, parks, and a few museums are among them. To discover free hotspots close by, check with the regional tourist agency or utilize a Wi-Fi locator app.

Wi-Fi portable devices:

Renting a pocket Wi-Fi or portable Wi-Fi device is an additional alternative for internet access. These gadgets provide a safe internet connection wherever you go and let you connect several devices at once. You may reserve portable Wi-Fi rental services in Rome in advance or when you arrive in the city.

Computer cafés:

There are still a few internet cafes in Rome even if they are not as prevalent as they once were. These places charge a fee for access to computers and internet connection. If you need to use a computer or print papers for any reason, these may be helpful.

Roaming:

You may use your mobile internet and make calls while in Rome if your mobile network carrier provides reasonable roaming pricing. However, keep in mind that there may be roaming fees, particularly if you use a lot of data. Before leaving, speak with your provider to learn about the expenses and available choices.

It's important to remember to use care while accessing sensitive information or doing online transactions when utilizing public Wi-Fi networks. Consider employing a virtual private network (VPN) for encryption and protection to safeguard the security of your personal data.

Having access to the internet will improve your trip to Rome since it will make it easier for you to keep in touch, get about, and find useful information.

Medical and Health Services

It's crucial to be ready and knowledgeable about the health and medical services offered in Rome before visiting. Here are some details to keep you healthy and take care of any medical requirements:

Consider purchasing travel insurance that includes medical coverage before your trip. In the event of any unanticipated medical emergency or health-related concerns, this guarantees your financial protection.

Medical Resources:

A variety of medical facilities, including public and private hospitals, clinics, and pharmacies, are available in Rome's well-developed healthcare system.

Public hospitals provide emergency care and treatment, but it's crucial to be aware that there may be communication hurdles and that waiting periods might vary.

In general, private hospitals and clinics provide more individualized treatment and have lower wait times. Additionally, they could employ personnel who are bilingual in English and/or other languages.

Pharmacies:

In Rome, pharmacies are referred to as "Farmacia." Look for the green cross sign outside the pharmacies.

The majority of pharmacies include trained staff members who can help with minor illnesses, dispense over-the-counter drugs, and provide guidance on common health conditions.

It's crucial to have enough of any required drugs or prescriptions with you on your vacation since you can often buy prescription medications in pharmacies in Italy.

Services for Emergencies:

To contact the ambulance service in an emergency, use the 112 emergency number in Europe.

You may also go straight to the emergency room of the closest hospital (Pronto Soccorso) if you need urgent medical care.

Vaccinations for Travel:

Make sure your usual vaccines are current before departing for Rome.

Additional immunizations or preventative measures can be advised depending on your place of origin and the length of your stay. For tailored guidance, speak with your medical professional or a travel health facility.

Health precautions in general:

To guarantee safe drinking water, sip on bottled water or use a water filter.

Wash your hands often, particularly before meals, to maintain excellent hygiene.

Wear sunscreen, a hat, and sunglasses to shield yourself from the sun, especially during the hot summer months.

When purchasing food from street sellers, exercise caution and make sure it is freshly made and cooked to perfection.

Carrying a small first-aid kit with basic supplies like bandages, painkillers, antiseptic wipes, and any necessary prescription prescriptions is advised. Prior to your journey, don't forget to review the travel warnings and recommendations issued by the government of your nation or the appropriate health authorities.

You may enjoy your time in Rome while preserving excellent health and having access to suitable medical services if required by being ready, being informed, and taking the essential steps.

BEYOND THE TOURIST

Trastevere:Bohemian Neighborhood

On Rome's west bank of the Tiber River sits Trastevere, a thriving and artistic area. Trastevere, which is well-known for its congested streets, vibrant architecture, and energetic atmosphere, provides a distinctive and genuine Roman experience. What to anticipate in this attractive area is as follows:

Investigating Trastevere
Start your tour of Trastevere by strolling through the neighborhood's charming streets,

which are lined with ancient buildings, ivy-covered walls, and cobblestone pathways. The best way to explore the neighborhood's peculiar old-world charm is on foot.

Trastevere's Santa Maria Square

Piazza di Santa Maria in Trastevere, a bustling plaza overshadowed by the beautiful Basilica of Santa Maria in Trastevere, is the center of Trastevere. This spectacular church, which is noted for its brilliant mosaics and lovely interior, was built in the fourth century.

Nightlife and Dining:

Trastevere is well known for its thriving eating scene, which has a variety of classic Roman trattorias, inviting osterias, hip pubs, and attractive cafés. Aperitivos, local wines, and delectable Roman food are all available in the neighborhood's vibrant taverns and busy squares at night.

Entertainment on the streets:

You may often see street performers, singers, and painters showing their skills as you walk around Trastevere. The area has a creative, bohemian feel that draws performers and artists, enhancing its distinctive character.

Secret Treasures and Creative Studios:

There are many undiscovered treasures in Trastevere, such as secret courtyards, artisan workshops, and art studios. Spend some time exploring the side streets to find local craftspeople, artists, and artisans at work.

Porta Portese's Sunday Market:

Do not miss the renowned Porta Portese flea market in Trastevere if you are in Rome on a Sunday. One of Rome's biggest and most well-liked marketplaces, it offers a vast selection of vintage goods, antiquities, apparel, accessories, and more.

The Farnesina Villa

Visit the magnificent Renaissance-style Villa Farnesina in Trastevere. This palace is a must-see for art fans due to its beautiful murals by well-known painters like Raphael.

Testaccio: Authentic Roman Experience

Rome's Testaccio area provides visitors with an immersive and genuine Roman experience. For those looking for an adventure off the beaten road, Testaccio is a must-visit because of its rich history, authentic food, and neighborhood feel. What to anticipate in this lively area is as follows:

Market at Testaccio:

Visit the bright and busy Testaccio Market as your first stop on your excursion. A large range of fresh fruit, meats, cheeses, and other regional goods are available here. Roman dishes may be sampled here, and you can also meet locals.

Traditional Roman food

Traditional Roman food is well-known in Testaccio. Don't pass up the chance to sample traditional foods like Roman-style pizza, carbonara (pasta with egg, cheese, and pancetta), and cacio e pepe (pasta with cheese and black pepper). Numerous trattorias and osterias that offer traditional Roman cuisine can be found in the area.

Contemporary Art Museum MACRO Testaccio: Pay a visit to the modern art gallery MACRO Testaccio. This museum, housed in a former slaughterhouse, displays creations by Italian and foreign artists. Immerse yourself in Rome's contemporary art scene by exploring the exhibits.

Testaccio, Monte

A remarkable ancient site called Monte Testaccio is nearby. It is a man-made hill built of pieces of old Roman amphorae. Learn about the hill's history and importance to Roman trade and commerce by taking a stroll around it.

Urban art
The street art movement in Testaccio is renowned for its energy. The neighborhood's walls are covered with vibrant murals and graffiti that you'll see as you walk about. Spend some time appreciating the urban art and taking some interesting pictures.

Cemetery in Testaccio:
A serene and noteworthy historical cemetery in Testaccio's Protestant Cemetery. John Keats and Percy Shelley are among the notable poets, authors, and painters whose last resting places are there. Visit this peaceful cemetery and take in the lovely sculptures and tombstones.

Entertainment at night:
A vibrant nightlife scene can be found in Testaccio, especially in and around Via di Monte Testaccio. There are several pubs, clubs, and live music venues in the neighborhood where you can spend the evening with locals and take in the vibrant nightlife of Rome.

Wine and food tours:
Take part in a Testaccio food or wine tour to learn more about the region's cuisine. These trips often include stops at local eateries, Roman specialties to sample, and historical and cultural insights about the city.

Away from the bustle of the city center, Testaccio provides a genuine and full Roman experience. This area has much to offer everyone, whether you like cuisine, art, or history. For a really unforgettable time in Rome, immerse yourself in the local culture, savor traditional food, and uncover Testaccio's hidden jewels.

Aventine Hill: A Relaxing Getaway

Rome's Aventine Hill is a serene and lovely area that provides a pleasant escape from the busy city center. Aventine Hill, which is located between the Tiber River and the Circus Maximus, is renowned for its tranquil environment, lovely gardens, and breathtaking views. What can you look forward to when visiting this wonderful area?

Giardino degli Aranci (Orange Garden):
The Orange Garden, a delightful park famed for its verdant greens and aromatic orange trees, is a great place to start your journey of Aventine Hill. Enjoy a leisurely walk around the garden's paths while basking in the shade of the trees and taking in the mesmerizing panoramic views of Rome, which include the dome of St. Peter's Basilica.

Keyhole View of the Dome of St. Peter:
Visit the Priory of the Knights of Malta atop Aventine Hill for a one-of-a-kind and unforgettable vantage point. The view of St. Peter's Basilica in the distance is well framed as you look through the keyhole of the priory's entry gate, producing a breathtaking scene.

Basilica of Santa Sabina:
A historic and stunning church in Rome is the Santa Sabina Basilica. This well-preserved church, which dates to the fifth century, has gorgeous architectural elements and magnificent mosaics. Enter to take in the peaceful ambiance and the antiquated artworks.

(Parco Savello) Savello Park
Savello Park is a serene and tranquil green area next to the Orange Garden. This undiscovered treasure has a lovely rose garden and sweeping views of Rome. It's the perfect place for a leisurely stroll, a picnic, or just to relax and take in the peace.

Monasteries and Churches:
There are several churches and monasteries atop Aventine Hill, each with a distinct beauty and historical value. Discover the Basilica of Santa Prisca, Sant'Anselmo all'Aventino, and other sacred locations to savor their aesthetic design and meditative atmosphere.

Maximus the Circus
The famous Circus Maximus, a former Roman chariot race track, is just a short stroll from Aventine Hill. Even though the site is now largely in ruins, one may nevertheless imagine its grandeur and discover its intriguing history. Imagine the thrill of the old Roman games as you wander over the historic track.
Walking on dates and taking pictures:
The calm alleys, quaint passageways, and picturesque vistas of Aventine Hill provide many chances for romantic strolls and photography. Capture the elegance of the area's buildings, beautiful landscaping, and breathtaking views, and take in the tranquility.
You may enjoy a calm getaway surrounded by breathtaking vistas and a feeling of solitude on Aventine Hill, which provides a welcome break from the rush and bustle of Rome. Take your time to discover the neighborhood's quiet nooks, take use of its parks, and soak in the peaceful atmosphere that makes Aventine Hill one of the most beautiful neighborhoods in Rome.

Monti: The Hipster Haven

Rome's Monti district has developed a reputation as a hipster paradise because it is thriving and fashionable. Monti provides a distinctive and varied experience with its creative flare, bohemian ambiance, and independent businesses. What to expect to discover in this trendy area is as follows:

Vintage stores and artisan shops:
The strong artisan community and antique shopping in Monti are well-known. Discover independent boutiques, vintage apparel shops, and artisan workshops by exploring the neighborhood's winding alleyways. These places sell one-of-a-kind clothes, handcrafted jewelry, and crafts.

Market on Monti Street (Mercatomonti):
The Monti Street Market, a well-liked weekend market conducted in the area, should not be missed. Local designers, vintage apparel, handcrafted accessories, and artisanal goods are on display at this market. It's a fantastic location to discover uncommon finds and support regional artists and business owners.

Unique bars and cafés:
There are several oddball cafés and bars in Monti, all of which have a relaxed and artistic atmosphere. You may choose from a variety of venues to suit your taste, from quaint book

cafés to chic cocktail bars. Sip on homemade drinks, read a book, or enjoy a cup of exquisite coffee while you take in the bohemian vibe of the area.

Galleries and displays of art

Numerous modern art galleries and exhibition venues can be found in Monti. Attend art openings, learn about regional and international artists, and get fully immersed in the neighborhood's thriving art scene. Keep an eye out for the area's frequent pop-up galleries and art events.

Hotspots for foodies and trendy eateries:

The culinary culture in Monti is broad and includes hip eateries, wine bars, and gastronomic attractions. Enjoy a range of cuisines, including fusion delicacies from across the world and classic Roman fare. Monti offers a variety of eating options, including quaint trattorias, fine dining establishments, and delicious street cuisine.

Place of the Madonna of the Mountains:

The center of the community, Piazza della Madonna dei Monti, is a bustling and sociable meeting spot. Get a drink or some gelato at one of the outside cafés, meet some residents and other tourists, and take in the lively spirit of the area.

Art Walk at Monti

Discover the street art and murals of Monti by going on a self-guided art tour. The area is decorated with vibrant and thought-provoking artworks, which further enhances its bohemian and artistic vibe. Discover undiscovered artistic treasures by exploring the streets and alleyways.

By Night in Monti:

Monti comes alive at night with concerts and events held at its taverns and live music venues. Discover the lively nightlife in the area, see a live performance by a band or DJ, and take in the cool, alternative vibe.

For those looking for unique and creative experiences in Rome, Monti is the appropriate location because of its renown as a hipster stronghold. For a unique visit to this colorful area of the city, explore its independent stores, socialize with the local creative scene, and experience the neighborhood's bohemian character.

EUR: Fascist-era Buildings

The Rome neighborhood known as EUR (Esposizione Universale di Roma) is renowned for its stunning architecture from the fascist period. Benito Mussolini's fascist dictatorship built EUR in the 1930s with the intention of showcasing the majesty and strength of the time. Today, it serves as a distinctive architectural reminder of the time. Here are some prominent examples of European architecture from the fascist era:

Italian Civilization Palace (Colosseo Quadrato): The Square Colosseum, also known as the Palazzo della Civiltà Italiana, is perhaps EUROPE's most recognizable structure. A sequence of arches and columns are part of its imposing design, which is evocative of early Roman construction. It presently serves as a renowned office space and has come to represent the neighborhood.

House of Congress Building:
Another notable structure in EUR is the Palazzo dei Congressi. It displays the era's colossal architectural style with its huge curving facade and graceful lines. It now serves as a venue for gatherings, conferences, and exhibits.

Palace of the Posts
The Post Office Palace, also known as the Palazzo delle Poste, is an impressive example of fascist-era design. Sculptures and reliefs depicting the principles of the fascist

dictatorship decorate its massive exterior. It still serves as a post office and is interesting to see for its amazing architectural features.

Museum of Roman Civilization:
In addition to housing a sizable collection of Roman antiquities, the Museo della Civiltà Romana in EUR also has noteworthy buildings from the fascist period. A grand entryway embellished with fascist symbols and ornamental elements can be seen on the museum building itself.

INA Office Building:
The National Institute for Social Insurance initially had its headquarters at the Palazzo Uffici dell'INA, currently known as the Palazzo INPS. The rationalist architectural design that was popular during the fascist period is seen in its symmetrical layout and lofty windows.

Obelisk of the Italian Forum:
The Obelisco del Foro Italico is noteworthy even though it is not a part of the EUR area since it exemplifies the fascist era's architectural style. This massive obelisk, which stands in the Foro Italico sports complex, is ornamented with reliefs and motifs honoring fascism and Italian athletics.

In order to fully appreciate the fascist-era structures at EUR, it is crucial to examine them historically and recognize how they relate to a complicated and contentious era of Italian history. The splendor of EUR's architecture serves as a reminder of the city's architectural variety and provides a window into the goals and objectives of the fascist dictatorship.

Garbatella: A Cute Residential Neighborhood

A lovely residential neighborhood called Garbatella may be found in Rome's south. Garbatella provides a particular experience for those seeking to see a different side of the city because of its unusual architecture, strong feeling of community, and vibrant environment. Here are some of this lovely neighborhood's highlights:

Historical Buildings
Architecture in Garbatella is well known for being distinctive and vibrant. The area was built as a garden city in the early 20th century and has low-rise structures with balconies, arches, and beautiful green courtyards. Take a leisurely walk around Garbatella's streets to take in the charming features and exquisite

architecture of the many structures, each of which has its own unique personality.

Girolamo Matteotti Square

The neighborhood's primary meeting spot is Piazza Girolamo Matteotti, Garbatella's principal plaza. It is surrounded by cafés, restaurants, and stores and has a lovely fountain. Sip some coffee and take in the local scene while people-watching or enjoying a cup of coffee.

Market in the neighborhood (Mercato di Via Ostiense):

On Via Ostiense in Garbatella, there is a thriving local market. You may explore a huge selection of fresh foods, regional goods, and home goods here. Enjoy the colorful atmosphere, chat with the sellers, and indulge in some delectable regional food.

Green Spaces and Community Gardens:

In addition to offering people tranquil getaways and a feeling of nature in the midst of the city, Garbatella is renowned for its various communal gardens and green areas. To appreciate the peace and beauty of these lush havens, take a walk through Parco Nemorense or tour the Garbatella Gardens (Orti di via Caffaro).

Park at Caffarella:

Caffarella Park, a sizable natural preserve next to Garbatella, provides a tranquil retreat from the city. Enjoy a picnic in the middle of nature while exploring the park's meadows, walking paths, and old Roman ruins.

Osterias and trattorias:

There are several trattorias and osterias in Garbatella where you may enjoy authentic Roman food and feel the warmth of Italian hospitality. Enjoy traditional fare including pasta, cacio e pepe, and carbonara with a glass of local wine.

Azzurro Scipioni Film:

Visit Garbatella's Cinema Azzurro Scipioni if you like watching movies. This lovely independent theater offers a carefully chosen variety of arthouse movies and offers a distinctive cultural experience.

Festivals and events held nearby:

Every year, Garbatella organizes a number of festivals and activities that unite the neighborhood in joy. Keep a look out for occasions that highlight regional customs, music, cuisine, and artistic performances, such the Sagra di San Michele and the Festival di Cinema Popolare.

Garbatella is a hidden treasure worth discovering during your trip to Rome because of its endearing residential ambience, remarkable architecture, and feeling of community. Discover the distinctive character of the area, engage with the residents, and take pleasure in the relaxed pace of life in this charming area of the city.

Ostiense Street Art and Culture

Rome's flourishing Ostiense area is well-known for its burgeoning cultural offerings and street art culture. This historically industrial region, next to the Ostiense railway station, has evolved into a center for creative expression. Here are some of the city of Ostiense's cultural and street art highlights:

Mural Street Art:
The walls, buildings, and often even whole facades of Ostiense are covered with stunning street art paintings. Discover colorful and thought-provoking artworks by regional and international artists by taking a stroll around the streets. The area's vibrant and creative character is reflected in the street art culture, which is always evolving.
Testaccio macro

In Ostiense, there is a museum of modern art called MACRO Testaccio. The museum, housed in a former slaughterhouse, hosts a variety of exhibits of modern and contemporary art. Discover the galleries, installations, and outdoor areas of the museum to fully immerse yourself in Ostiense's thriving art scene.

Montemartini Centrale

A unique museum called Centrale Montemartini is housed in a former power station. It creates a contrast of old and new components by fusing classical sculpture with commercial equipment. For lovers of art and history, the museum's creative approach delivers a stimulating experience.

Live performances of music:

Numerous live music venues and performance spaces can be found in Ostiense, where you can listen to music in a range of styles, including jazz, rock, techno, and experimental. For a night of live music and cultural activities, check out places like Monk Club and Circolo degli Artisti.

Market at Ostiense:

The Ostiense Market, a favorite hangout for foodies, is close to the Ostiense railway station. This crowded market has a large assortment of handcrafted goods, street food vendors, and fresh vegetables. Discover the market to taste regional specialties and take in the neighborhood's thriving culinary culture.

Cultural Festivals and Events:

Ostiense has a number of cultural events and festivals all year long, exhibiting the artistic and creative energy of the area. Watch for occasions like Open House Roma, where you may discover undiscovered architectural treasures, or the Ostiense Street Food Festival, which honors regional cuisine and culinary customs.

Various Bars and Cafés:

Numerous alternative pubs, cafés, and eateries that appeal to the neighborhood's creative community can be found in Ostiense. Find unique cafés, chic cocktail bars, and welcoming wine bars where you can relax, mingle, and take in the local ambiance.

Vintage stores and flea markets:

Street markets and antique stores are further attractions in Ostiense. Investigate the Mercato di Testaccio, a neighborhood market where you may purchase clothes, food, and home products. Visit the vintage stores in the area to locate one-of-a-kind clothing items and vintage treasures.

For fans of the arts, musicians, and those looking for a dynamic and creative experience in Rome, Ostiense is a must-visit location because of its street art, cultural attractions, and bustling environment. Discover hidden jewels, immerse yourself in the neighborhood's distinctive creative manifestations, and experience Ostiense's vibrant vitality.

ROME FOR FAMILIES

Family-friendly Attractions

Rome has a wide variety of activities and attractions geared at families with young tourists. The city offers chances for family-friendly educational and enjoyable activities, from historical sites to interactive museums. The following are some of Rome's finest family-friendly attractions:

Roman Forum and the Colosseum:
The famous Colosseum and Roman Forum are great places for students to learn about ancient history. To make the experience interesting and instructive, think about signing up for a guided tour created especially for families.
Children's Museum Explora:

Children's discovery and learning are the focus of the Explora Children's Museum. It has interactive displays that encourage imagination, problem-solving, and scientific research. Kids may take part in a variety of activities, such as building structures and making art.

Bioparco (Zoo of Rome)

Bioparco, a well-kept zoo that offers a family-friendly and educational experience, is situated in Villa Borghese. Explore the park on foot, get up close to a variety of animals, and take in animal performances and demonstrations.

Gardens at Villa Borghese:

Families may relax, have a picnic, and engage in outdoor activities in the expansive green area provided by Villa Borghese Gardens. Visit the playgrounds, rent bicycles or pedal boats, or explore the park's attractions, such as the Bioparco and the Casa del Cinema.

Rome's Time Elevator:

An immersive multimedia experience called The Time Elevator takes users on a virtual tour of Rome's past. It provides an interesting and enjoyable method to learn about the history of the city using a blend of 3D graphics, motion simulators, and special effects.

Hollywood World:

Theme park Cinecittà World is devoted to the film and entertainment industries. It offers guests the chance to experience the enchantment of the movies via exhilarating rides, live performances, and film sets. There is entertainment for every member of the family, including 4D attractions and roller coasters.

Roma's Bioparco:
Near Villa Borghese is a smaller zoo called Bioparco di Roma. It is home to a diverse variety of creatures, including reptiles, giraffes, elephants, and lions. Children may enjoy a playground area and educational events at the zoo.

Gladiator Academy
Consider attending a Gladiator School for a fun and engaging experience. Children may don gladiator costumes, study Roman fighting strategies, and engage in fictitious combat. This practical experience offers a fascinating and instructive look into Roman history.

Catacombs of Rome:
A trip to the Rome Catacombs can fascinate older kids. It might be fascinating and instructive to explore the subterranean tunnels while learning about the burial customs of the early Christians.

Ice-cream sampling

Go on an ice cream sampling journey and indulge in Rome's world-famous gelato. Visit classic gelaterias and indulge in a leisurely walk around the streets of the city while sampling a range of tastes.

Rome's family-friendly sites include a variety of historical, cultural, entertaining, and outdoor activities that are appropriate for visitors of all ages. Rome offers a variety of activities to make lifelong experiences for the whole family, whether it's visiting ancient ruins, participating in interactive museums, or just taking in the city's parks and culinary offerings.

Playgrounds and Parks

There are several parks and playgrounds in Rome where families may relax, participate in outdoor activities, and allow children to play. These parks include open spaces, play areas, and a range of recreational amenities. The following parks and playgrounds are important ones in Rome:

Gardens at Villa Borghese:
In the center of Rome, there is a sizable park called Villa Borghese. It has expansive gardens,

jogging trails, and outdoor leisure spaces. Families may go to the playgrounds, have a picnic, rent bicycles or pedal boats, or visit sites like the Bioparco (the Rome Zoo) and the Casa del Cinema.

House Ada:
The second-largest park in Rome, Villa Ada, provides plenty of room for families to enjoy outdoor sports. The park has picnic spaces, a lake, and walking routes. Kids may ride bikes, play on the playgrounds, or play sports like volleyball and soccer.

The Pamphilj Villa
One of Rome's biggest parks, Villa Pamphilj, provides a lot of room for families to relax. Large lawns, walking trails, and picnic places with shade may be found in the park. Kids may ride bikes, visit the playgrounds, and even take a pony ride.

Park of the Acquedottis:
Parco degli Acquedotti, a picturesque park outside of Rome, is home to many historic Roman aqueducts. Families may enjoy the ancient buildings while taking a leisurely bike ride or stroll along the pathways. The park provides open areas for picnics and leisure pursuits.

Hill Janiculum (Gianicolo):

Rome can be seen in all directions from the lovely hilltop park known as Janiculum Hill. Families may enjoy a picnic with a view, a leisurely walk along the trails, and time for their kids to play in the open areas. A modest children's playground is also included in the park.

The Caffarella Park

A sizable park called Parco della Caffarella is next to Appian Way Regional Park. It has a lot of open green space, including walking trails and meadows. Families may have a picnic, engage in outdoor activities, and take in the park's breathtaking scenery.

Park of Memories:

A smaller park called Parco Nemorense is located in the Nomentano district. For the amusement of kids and teens, it has a playground area, a basketball court, and a skate park. The park is a wonderful location for a leisurely family excursion.

The Park at Victory:

A park in the Monteverde district called Parco della Vittoria has a number of amenities for families. Playgrounds, athletic fields, and picnic spaces are included. Families may enjoy outdoor pursuits or just unwind in the serene park setting.

Families may enjoy the outdoors, participate in fun activities, and make lifelong memories at these parks and playgrounds in Rome. These green areas provide recreational opportunities for people of all ages while offering a welcome respite from the bustle of the city, whether it be via garden exploration, playground play, or a leisurely picnic.

Children's-Oriented museums and Exhibits

There are a number of kid-friendly museums and exhibitions in Rome that appeal to younger tourists and provide engaging activities. These museums and exhibitions are intended to pique kids' interests, inspire their creativity, and make learning enjoyable. Here are some museums and attractions in Rome that are kid-friendly:

Children's Museum Explora:
Explora is a specialized children's museum that provides a selection of engaging exhibits and kid-friendly activities. Children may explore a variety of topics—including science, technology, art, and daily life—hands-on. The

museum promotes play-based learning, creativity, and problem-solving.

House of Congress Building:
Children's programs and temporary exhibitions are held in the Palazzo dei Congressi. These displays offer young visitors a distinctive and interesting experience, ranging from immersive art installations to interactive scientific demonstrations.

Children's Museum of Rome (Museo dei Bambini di Roma):
Another interactive museum created for kids is Museo dei Bambini di Roma. It has a wide range of exhibitions that concentrate on many facets of life, including the environment, health, and society. Children may take part in role-playing activities, explore, and learn about a variety of subjects.

Astronomical Museum and Planetarium (Planetarium):
For young space lovers, the Planetarium and Astronomical Museum in Rome offers an engaging experience. With the help of interactive displays, planetarium performances, and educational seminars, kids may learn about the marvels of the cosmos.

Technotown:
In Villa Torlonia, there is a museum dedicated to technology called Technotown. Children are

introduced to many facets of technology, such as robotics, programming, and multimedia arts, via interactive exhibitions and workshops. Kids may explore the digital world and take part in hands-on activities.

Zoological Museum:
Children learn about the richness of the natural world at the University of Rome "La Sapienza" Museum of Zoology, which exhibits a broad variety of animal species. Children get the chance to learn about many animals, habitats, and the value of conservation.

National Pasta Museum
The "Museo Nazionale delle Paste Alimentari," or "National Museum of Pasta," studies the development and cultural importance of pasta in Italy. Children may explore interactive exhibitions, try out various pasta forms, and even take part in pasta-making activities.

Rome's kid-friendly museums and attractions provide young visitors fun and instructive experiences. They encourage hands-on learning, pique children's interest, and provide them the chance to explore a variety of topics in a fun and engaging manner. These attractions, which include a variety of scientific, technology, art, and cultural themes, are likely to capture kids' imaginations and provide priceless memories.

Child-Friendly Cafés & Restaurants

Families with children may find a range of kid-friendly eateries and cafés in Rome. These businesses provide a pleasant environment, kid-friendly meals, and often feature facilities or entertainment for youngsters. These suggested eateries and coffee shops in Rome are family-friendly:

Roscioli Coffee and Pastry:
Roscioli Caffè Pasticceria is a well-known café that offers a variety of pastries, sweets, and light meals and is situated close to Campo de' Fiori. Children may savor delectable sweets including pastries, cookies, and gelato in a welcoming environment.

Pizza restaurant L'Isola della Pizza:
Family-friendly pizza restaurant L'Isola della Pizza is close to the Vatican City. It provides a cheerful atmosphere and a cuisine with a selection of pizzas, pasta dishes, and family-friendly entrees. High chairs and a kids' play area are also available at the restaurant.

The San Crispino Gelato:

A well-known gelateria that provides a large variety of mouthwatering gelato flavors is Il Gelato di San Crispino. The staff often accommodates young customers, and children will enjoy experiencing the many tastes.

Theodore Testaccio:
Popular family-friendly dining establishment Felice a Testaccio is well-known for serving food from Rome. It offers classic fare including carbonara, spaghetti, and fried artichokes. Families will enjoy the cozy and welcoming ambiance at the restaurant.

Piperno's Ristorante:
Family-friendly, Jewish-Roman food is the focus of Ristorante Piperno, which is situated in the Jewish Ghetto. There are many different foods available, including pasta, seafood, and customary Roman-Jewish delicacies. Families with little children will feel at home at the restaurant.

The imperial pasta
Near the Trevi Fountain is a restaurant called Pasta Imperiale, which specializes in meals with fresh pasta. While parents indulge in classic Roman cuisine, kids may eat their favorite pasta shapes with a selection of sauces.

Sant'Eustachio Coffee:
Rome's famous Caffè Sant'Eustachio is renowned for its excellent coffee. Families may

indulge on pastries and sweets while sipping hot chocolate or coffee. The café features a cozy, friendly atmosphere that is ideal for families.

Fabi Gelateria:
One of Rome's oldest and most well-known gelaterias is Gelateria Fassi. Kids will enjoy sampling the many different varieties of gelato and indulging in traditional Italian sweets like affogato and granita.

The Margutta Restaurant:
A vegetarian and vegan restaurant called Il Margutta RistorArte is located near Piazza del Popolo. It provides a wonderful plant-based cuisine that is kid-friendly. The eatery's laid-back ambiance and frequent art shows enhance the eating experience.

Rome's family-friendly eateries and coffee shops provide a warm atmosphere, delectable cuisine, and kid-friendly menu selections. These places provide a pleasurable eating experience for the entire family, whether it is savoring classic Roman foods, enjoying gelato, or indulging in pastries and sweets.

Children's Sweet Treats and Gelato

There are many delicious alternatives to choose from in Rome when it comes to gelato and sweets for kids. These suggestions will definitely satisfy your kid's sweet tooth:

Della Palma Gelateria:
In a well-known gelateria next to the Pantheon, called Gelateria della Palma, you may choose from a wide variety of gelato tastes. Kids will enjoy selecting their favorite flavors from among the many colored gelato tubs that are available.

Giolitti:
Near the Trevi Fountain, Giolitti is a gelateria renowned for its thick and creamy gelato. Your youngster may design their own delicious gelato creation using a selection of flavors and toppings.

The San Crispino Gelato:
Another outstanding gelateria that is adored by both residents and visitors is Il Gelato di San Crispino, which was already highlighted. Their gelato is created with premium ingredients and comes in a variety of traditional and unusual flavors that kids will love.

Regoli Pasticceria:
Rome's well-known Pasticceria Regoli has been a favorite among residents for more than a century. They provide a large assortment of

cakes, pastries, and other sweets that are ideal for kids. Try any of their biscotti varieties, sfogliatelle, or cannoli.

Pompi's Tiramisu:

The specialty dessert store Tiramisu by Pompi specializes in the traditional Italian dessert tiramisu. The varieties they provide range from conventional to strawberry to pistachio and other delights. The rich and creamy layers of this famous dessert will appeal to children.

In Le Levain:

A lovely bakery that specializes in French desserts is called Le Levain. Kids will like the exquisite variety of croissants, pain au chocolat, and other sweet goodies they have to offer.

Pastry Shop De Bellis:

In the Prati area, there is a family-run pastry store called Pasticceria De Bellis. They have a delectable selection of cookies, cakes, and pastries that are ideal for kids. Their Nutella-filled croissants, a child favorite, are not to be missed.

Gelato Fatamorgana:

The handmade gelato produced by Fatamorgana Gelato is renowned for being crafted with natural and organic ingredients. There is something for everyone because of the wide range of flavors they provide, including vegan and dairy-free alternatives.

Children will like the delicious selection of gelato and sweet snacks available at these gelaterias, pastry shops, and dessert establishments in Rome. These delights, which come in both traditional tastes and inventive combinations, are sure to delight your child's taste buds and leave them with long-lasting memories of their stay in Rome.

Kids' Entertainment and Activities

Rome has a variety of amusement and activities that are especially created to occupy and amuse children. Here are some recreational and entertainment choices for kids in Rome:

Bioparco (Zoo of Rome)
Families with young children love to visit Bioparco. It is housed at Villa Borghese and has a large collection of animals from all around the globe. Children may take pleasure in watching animals, going to animal feedings, and even participating in educational seminars. Rome's Time Elevator:

A virtual tour through Rome's history is provided with the immersive multimedia experience Time Elevator Rome. A 3D screen, motion chairs, and special effects are used to provide a fun and instructive trip for kids.

Water Park Hydromania:

Just outside of Rome, there is a water park called Hydromania that provides the ideal respite from the summer heat. For kids of all ages, it has wave pools, water slides, and other attractions.

Blue Magicland:

A theme park with a variety of kid-friendly rides and activities is called Rainbow Magicland, and it is not far from Rome. Children may stay delighted and thrilled with a variety of activities, including roller coasters and carousels.

Children's Museum Explora:

Children may learn by doing at the previously mentioned Explora Children's Museum. It provides engaging exhibitions and seminars that inspire kids to playfully explore science, art, and daily life.

Gardens at Villa Borghese:

Children may participate in a variety of activities in the spacious public park known as Villa Borghese Gardens. Families may take leisurely strolls, hire pedal boats, or bicycles and enjoy the stunning surroundings. A small zoo and playgrounds are also included in the park.

Gladiator Academy

In several locations in Rome, children may take part in fake gladiator fights while learning about the historical Roman gladiators. Children may go back in time and experience a little bit of ancient Rome during these engaging programs.

Children's Theatre of Rome:

Children's theater productions are presented at the Rome Children's Theatre. Children may take in live entertainment in a kid-friendly setting, such as puppet shows and plays.

Hollywood World:

An amusement park devoted to the movie industry is called Cinecittà World. It has rides and attractions based on well-known movies, making it an entertaining vacation spot for youngsters who like movies.

Small-scale park:

Scaled-down versions of well-known structures and monuments from all across Italy may be seen at Miniature Park, a unique attraction. Kids may explore the scaled-down replicas of famous locations, educating them about the rich architectural history of Italy.

Kids will have a memorable and delightful time in Rome thanks to these entertainment and activity alternatives. Children will find enough to engage them and amuse them during their visit to the Eternal City, from engaging museums to exhilarating amusement parks.

Practical Travel Advice for Traveling with kids

Taking a trip with kids may be enjoyable and memorable. Here are some helpful advice for traveling with kids to guarantee a smooth and fun trip:

Research kid-friendly activities, lodgings, and eateries before you go. Make a list of the places and activities your kids might like, and then adjust your agenda.

Be smart about your packing: Include necessities like diapers, baby wipes, extra clothing, food, and prescriptions. To keep kids entertained during travel and downtime, you should also think about carrying toys, books, and small technological gadgets.

202)

Select family-friendly lodging: Look for lodgings with kid-friendly features including cribs, high chairs, and play spaces. Think about booking a family suite at a hotel or apartment for additional room and comfort.

Maintain routine: Do your best to follow your child's normal schedule, which should include mealtimes and bedtimes. This may make children feel safer and more at ease in a strange setting.

Be adaptable: While having a plan is necessary, you should also be flexible with your schedule and be ready for unforeseen adjustments. Be prepared to modify your plans in light of the possibility that children may have different requirements or will tire more rapidly.

Plan frequent stops while touring to give kids a chance to relax and refuel. Look for playgrounds or parks where kids may run about and let off some steam.

Children should be included in the planning process by being given the opportunity to choose the activities or sights that interest them. They may become more enthusiastic and involved in the adventure as a result.

Safety first: Pay strict attention to your kids, particularly in busy places. Hold their hands while crossing busy streets and keep them in your line of sight at all times.

Carry water bottles and snacks so that your kids may stay hydrated and stimulated throughout the day. When required, this may provide speedy refreshments and help avoid meltdowns.

Traveling with kids may sometimes be difficult, so it's crucial to maintain your composure and patience. Be ready for unforeseen circumstances and address them in a constructive manner.

Just keep in mind that taking a family vacation may be a memorable experience. You may make the vacation successful and fun for the whole family by making plans in advance, being adaptable, and taking your child's needs into account.

NIGHTLIFE AND ENTERTAINMENT

Cocktail Lounges and Bars

Rome has a thriving bar and cocktail culture, with a variety of venues to accommodate different tastes and preferences. Here are a few well-known pubs and cocktail lounges to check out:

A hidden jewel in the heart of the city, the Jerry Thomas Speakeasy is renowned for its talented mixologists who create one-of-a-kind drinks. It's a well-liked destination for lovers of cocktails since it has a feel like a speakeasy from the days of Prohibition.

The Race Club is a chic cocktail bar with a sophisticated ambiance that is close to Piazza Navona. It provides a large range of beautifully created beverages. The bartenders are renowned for their meticulousness and mixological expertise.

Freni & Frizioni is a fashionable bar located in the Trastevere district that emanates an eclectic and hip air. It used to be a mechanic's shop. A wide range of beverages are available, including creative cocktails and an outstanding choice of beers.

Salotto 42 is a stylish lounge bar that is close to the Pantheon and is renowned for its opulent design and welcoming atmosphere. It specializes in offering a wide range of traditional and unique drinks, along with a variety of mouthwatering food.

Drink Kong: This well-known establishment in the Testaccio district mixes a distinctive fusion of Asian and Western elements to create a dynamic and varied ambiance. It's a terrific place for a night out since it offers a wide selection of cocktails and has DJ nights.

The Court: This rooftop bar at Palazzo Manfredi has stunning views of the Colosseum. Drink in the magnificent views and enchanted aura of this historical site while sipping on a cool beverage.

The Barber Shop is a speakeasy-style pub concealed in Trastevere that astounds guests with its secret entrance and cozy ambiance. The bar provides a variety of traditional and

206)

modern drinks, and the bartenders here are renowned for their inventive creations.

Stravinskij Bar is a part of the Hotel de Russie and is positioned in the center of Rome's upscale shopping area. A calm atmosphere to sample a variety of perfectly made cocktails in a chic setting is provided by the bar's attractive outside patio.

The Monti neighborhood's fashionable Barnum Café provides a welcoming and laid-back ambiance. It offers a wide variety of alcoholic beverages, including inventive cocktails and a wide range of spirits and liquors.

Fluid Bar & Lounge provides a chic and contemporary location for sipping cocktails and other beverages close to Piazza del Popolo. It has a varied menu with traditional drinks, original inventions, and a sizable wine selection.

These Rome pubs and cocktail lounges provide a variety of experiences, from traditional and elegant settings to cutting-edge and fashionable hangouts. Rome has a lot to offer those hoping to enjoy a delicious drink in a chic atmosphere, whether you're searching for a chic cocktail club or a young and dynamic pub.

NightClubs and Dance Locations

Rome offers a booming nightlife culture with a range of clubs and dance locations where you may party the night away to various musical genres. Here are a few of Rome's well-liked dance clubs and bars:

Goa Club is well-known for its underground electronic music scene and is situated in the Testaccio district of Rome. It draws a wide range of music lovers by hosting both local and foreign DJs.

Rashomon Club: A hip nightclub noted for its electronic and house music, Rashomon Club is located close to the Colosseum. It has many dance floors, each with a different atmosphere and musical genre.

The Monti neighborhood's Shari Vari Playhouse provides a distinctive and all-encompassing evening experience. The location features a blend of music, art, and performance, resulting in a memorable ambiance.

Akab Club is a well-known nightclub that draws in a wide variety of patrons. It is situated in the Esquilino neighborhood. Hip-hop, reggaeton, and pop songs are all mixed together, creating a dynamic and energizing ambiance.

Room 26: A sizable, upmarket nightclub in the Ostiense neighborhood, Room 26 is renowned for featuring top DJs and international performers. It offers a realistic dancing experience with its cutting-edge lighting and outstanding sound system.

Piper Club: Opened in the 1960s, Piper Club is a legendary nightclub in the Trastevere district. It features a variety of musical styles, including rock, pop, and indie, and throughout the years, many well-known performers have performed there.

Akab Club is a well-liked location for dancing and taking in a lively evening experience. It is close to Campo de' Fiori. There is something for everyone because of the several dance floors and varied music.

Planet Roma: A sizable nightclub with wide dance floors and a broad musical selection, Planet Roma is located close to Termini Station. It conducts themed events and parties that draw a vivacious and vivacious audience.

Ex Dogana: During the evening, this distinctive and varied cultural venue is transformed into a buzzing nightclub. It is a venue for a range of music events, including live, hip-hop, and electronic acts, and is situated in the San Lorenzo district.

In the heart of the city, there is a historic theater called Salone Margherita that also serves as a nightclub. It provides a variety of live music, DJ sets, and themed evenings to create an energetic and ethereal dancing environment.

Please be aware that Rome's nightlife scene is dynamic and that places may alter or develop over time. For the most recent details on events, dress standards, and admission requirements, visit their websites or local listings. Additionally, take your time carefully to educate yourself with local rules and laws governing drinking age limitations.

Concerts And Live Music

Rome boasts a thriving live music scene that offers a variety of places to take in live performances and concerts of all genres. Here are some of Rome's most well-liked locations for live music and concerts:

Auditorium Parco della Musica: This renowned music venue presents a range of programs, from jazz and current to opera and classical. There are many music venues there as well as an outdoor amphitheater, which offers great acoustics and a wide range of acts.

Opera, ballet, and classical music events are presented in the Teatro dell'Opera di Roma, often known as the Rome Opera House. It draws famous performers and fans of opera by presenting both conventional productions and fresh interpretations.

Jazz performers from all over the world perform in the yearly Villa Celimontana Jazz Festival, which takes place in the lovely location of the same name. Visitors may take in outdoor music in the picturesque setting of the park.

Alexanderplatz Jazz Club: Located in the core of Rome's old district, Alexanderplatz is a well-liked jazz venue renowned for its cozy atmosphere and outstanding performances. Live jazz performances, jam sessions, and sporadic blues and soul concerts are held there.

Big Mama: Since 1984, Rome has been home to this famous blues and jazz venue. It offers a warm and genuine environment for taking in live music and welcomes both established and up-and-coming musicians.

The Pigneto neighborhood's Lanificio 159 is a multipurpose venue that holds a range of events, such as live music concerts, DJ sets, and parties. It features a variety of musical styles, including electronic, indie, and alternative.

Monk Club: Located in the Trastevere district, Monk Club is a well-known live music venue that features regional as well as international musicians from a variety of musical genres. It boasts a lively atmosphere and a varied schedule of performances by DJs.

Rising Love: In the San Lorenzo district, this buzzing music establishment presents a variety of themed events, DJ sets, and live music performances. It provides a lively environment and a stage for up-and-coming acts.

Fonclea: Situated there. Rock, indie, jazz, and blues are performed live in the small, secluded venue Fonclea in the Lorenzo/Trieste neighborhood. It provides a laid-back environment and a stage for regional talent.

Black Market is a well-known pub and music venue that presents live music performances, DJ sets, and open mic nights. It is situated in the Monti area. It features a variety of musical styles, such as rock, punk, and alternative music.

Rome's live music scene may be rather diverse, so it's best to check the venue's website or local listings for details on forthcoming events, ticket availability, and any age limits. Additionally, it is advised to get tickets in advance for well-liked performances, particularly during the busiest travel seasons.

Theater and Performing Arts

Rome boasts a thriving theater and performing arts scene with several locations where you may see plays, theatrical productions, and other live acts. Here are a few of Rome's well-known theaters and performance spaces:

The Teatro di Roma, the city of Rome's official theater, offers a variety of theatrical productions, such as classic plays, modern plays, and experimental performances. There are several locations for it across the city, such as Teatro Argentina and Teatro India.

The Teatro dell'Angelo is a tiny, cozy theater close to Piazza Navona that presents a variety of modern theater, music, dance, and multimedia acts. It offers a stage for up-and-coming performers and creative shows.

The Teatro Sistina is a well-known theater that often presents musicals, comedies, and dramatic performances. It is situated close to Piazza Barberini. Its vast interior and lengthy history provide for an unforgettable theatrical experience.

The Teatro Quirino is a historic theater that can be found close to the Trevi Fountain. It hosts a variety of theatrical, dance, and musical acts. It has a lovely neoclassical exterior and a classy interior.

The Piccolo Eliseo Theatre is a tiny theater that hosts a variety of theatrical plays, comedic performances, and musical events. It is located close to Villa Borghese. It has a cozy atmosphere and welcomes both well-known and up-and-coming performers.

The Teatro Argentina is one of Rome's oldest theaters and presents a range of theatrical productions, from classic plays to modern plays. It has a lengthy history and has played home to several famous performers and directors.

The Teatro Valle is a historic theater of political and cultural importance that is close to the Pantheon. It holds a variety of theater productions, dance performances, and other creative events, often fostering social and cultural exchange.

Teatro India: A modern theater with a concentration on cutting-edge and

215)

experimental shows, Teatro India is located in the Ostiense area. It features performances in a range of performing arts, such as theater, dance, and multimedia.

The Teatro Ambra Jovinelli is a historic theater that can be found close to Termini Station. It has a varied schedule of theatrical shows, ranging from classic plays to modern pieces. It has a rich artistic history and an attractive interior.

The contemporary performing arts center Auditorium Conciliazione, which is close to the Vatican, organizes a range of activities, including theater productions, concerts, and dance performances. It has cutting-edge amenities and a flexible stage.

It's important to keep in mind that show and performance availability might change, so it's best to check the theater's website or local listings for the most recent details on schedules, ticket costs, and availability. Additionally, some performances could be in Italian, so it's important to find out whether there are any translations or subtitles in English for audience members who don't know Italian.

216)

Outdoor Theaters And Film Festivals

Rome has a wonderful collection of outdoor movie theaters and film festivals that let guests watch movies while stargazing and appreciate the craft of filmmaking. Here are a few of Rome's well-liked outdoor movie theaters and film festivals:

Open-Air Theaters:

Isola del Cinema: Situated on Tiber Island, Isola del Cinema is a well-known open-air theater that presents summertime film screenings, retrospectives, and special events. It offers a distinctive position with the Tiber River as a beautiful background.

Casa del theater: Located in the lovely Villa Borghese park, Casa del Cinema offers an outdoor theater where guests may take in movie showings and festivals all year long. Additionally, it conducts film-related conversations, seminars, and exhibits.

Arena di Campo Testaccio: During the summer, this ancient amphitheater in the Testaccio district is converted into an outdoor movie theater. It shows a variety of modern releases, indie films, and old movies.

Cinecittà Estivo: Located inside the Cinecittà Studios complex, Cinecittà Estivo provides summertime outdoor moviegoing. It features a wide variety of movies, such as Italian classics, blockbusters from across the world, and independent films.

Festivals of film:

One of the most well-known film festivals in Italy is the Rome Film Fest, which takes place every year in October. It draws renowned directors and performers from all over the globe with its broad range of foreign films, debuts, and retrospectives.

Cinema America Occupato: A distinctive film festival that supports independent cinema, Cinema America Occupato is held in the summer. It shows a range of movies, such as experimental movies, short movies, and documentaries.

The films for a younger audience are the main emphasis of this part of the Rome Film Festival, Alice nella Città. It provides a varied selection of foreign children's and young adult films, as well as seminars and other film-related events.

The Rome indie Film Festival, sometimes referred to as RIFF, honors indie cinema and up-and-coming talent. It offers independent filmmakers a platform by showcasing a variety of genres, including feature films, documentaries, and short films.

RIFFaRoma is an annual film festival that emphasizes experimental and creative filmmaking. It offers a variety of cutting-edge and avant-garde movies from all over the globe, encouraging discussion and inquiry into the world of cinema.

Please be aware that open-air movie theaters and film festivals may change their times and locations. For the most recent facts on screenings, ticket costs, and event specifics, it is advised to consult the official websites or local listings.

Late-Night Restaurants and Foodie Hotspots

Rome is renowned for its thriving culinary culture, and you can satiate your appetites at any time of the day or night at one of the many late-night restaurants and gastronomic hotspots there. Here are some suggestions for late-night eating establishments and culinary experiences in Rome:

Late-night eating is popular in Trastevere, a bohemian district. There are several trattorias, pizzerias, and wine bars where you may enjoy authentic Roman cuisine in a fun environment.

Testaccio: Home to a number of late-night eating establishments and renowned for its traditional Roman food. Discover the neighborhood's trattorias and osterias to sample regional specialties like cacio e pepe and carbonara.

Campo de' Fiori: With a thriving nightlife, this busy piazza comes to life at night. It's a terrific place for late-night eating and people-watching since there are pubs and restaurants offering both Italian and other cuisines.

Monti: This fashionable area is well-known for its stylish clubs and restaurants. Discover specialized eateries that serve a mix of traditional and cutting-edge cuisine, including street food, gourmet burgers, and fusion specialties, as you explore the winding alleyways.

Pigneto: A favorite hangout for the city's youthful and creative population, Pigneto has a variety of trendy eateries, wine bars, and cocktail lounges. You may delight in inventive cuisine and take in the colorful environment here.

Mercato Centrale Roma is an open-late food court that can be found close to Termini Station. There are several different shops and restaurants there, serving anything from pizza and pasta to gelato and upscale snacks.

Jewish Ghetto: Known for its authentic Roman-Jewish food, the Jewish Ghetto is a historic area. A few of the local eateries provide a distinctive dining experience by serving kosher food and staying open late.

Rome is well-known for its gelato, and many of its gelaterias are open late. Give yourself a treat by getting a scoop or two of exquisite gelato from a famous gelato store like Giolitti, Fatamorgana, or La Romana.

Food Tours & Experiences: Taking part in a food tour or experience is a terrific opportunity to explore off-the-beaten-path restaurants and sample a range of regional cuisine. In Rome, a number of businesses provide nighttime meal excursions, bar crawls, and wine tastings.

Food Markets: Stock up on fresh vegetables, cheese, cured meats, and other treats by going to the neighborhood food markets, such Mercato di Testaccio or Mercato di Campo de' Fiori, throughout the day. With these supplies, you may make your own late-night meal or have a picnic in one of Rome's lovely squares.

When eating late at night, it's a good idea to verify the opening times and, if required, make appointments since certain locations can have limited availability or demand reservations in advance.

Guided Tours & Activities in Rome at Night

Roman structures that are lighted at night and a thriving nightlife provide for a fantastic experience while exploring the city. Here are some activities and trips that can let you see Rome's splendor after dark:

Join a guided walking tour at night to see Rome's famous sights against the backdrop of the starry night. While touring the city with professional guides, you'll see sights like the Colosseum, Trevi Fountain, Pantheon, and Piazza Navona while learning about its past and lore.

Night Segway Tours: Take a nighttime guided segway tour through Rome's streets. Ride a segway and discover the city's top attractions, including the Spanish Steps, Piazza di Spagna, and Castel Sant'Angelo.

Twilight Bike Tours: Set out on a narrated bike tour as the sun sets through Rome's charming streets and plazas. While pedaling around the city at twilight, you'll pass well-known sites including the Roman Forum, Capitoline Hill, and Circus Maximus.

Evening Food Tours: Take a food tour with a guide to see Rome's gastronomic wonders at night. While meandering through lovely areas like Trastevere or the Jewish Ghetto, try local wines, typical Roman snacks, and foods like pizza, pasta, and gelato.

Rome Rooftop Bar Tours: Join a guided tour to see the city's stunning rooftop pubs and terraces. Drink in panoramic views of the Colosseum, St. Peter's Basilica, or the Roman skyline while your guide provides enlightening commentary.

Nighttime River Cruises: Board a riverboat down the Tiber River for a unique view of Rome's sights lit up at night. Enjoy a tranquil evening on the lake as you pass famous locations including St. Peter's Basilica, Castel Sant'Angelo, and the Vatican.

Join a ghost or mystery tour of Rome at night for a fascinating and perhaps unsettling experience. Your guide will offer spine-tingling tales and folklore as you explore the city's sinister legends, haunting locations, and unsolved mysteries.

Opera & Classical Music Performances: Spend an evening at the opera or attend a performance at one of Rome's iconic venues to fully immerse yourself in the world of classical music. Experience opera companies, choirs, and orchestras performing well-known pieces by Verdi and Puccini, whose immortal melodies will be brought to life.

Nighttime Vatican Tours: Take part in an after-hours or nighttime tour to see the Vatican Museums and Sistine Chapel in a new way. By avoiding the crowds, you may enjoy the art and architecture in a more peaceful setting while learning from knowledgeable experts.

Night photography tours: Take a guided photography trip to capture Rome's splendor at night. While visiting the city with a professional photographer, pick out tips and tricks for getting beautiful evening pictures of the city's landmarks and secret spots.

Always double-check these tours' schedules and times in advance since they could change throughout the year. To ensure your place and make the most of your nighttime exploration of Rome, it is advised to make reservations in advance for certain trips.

SPORT AND RECREATION

Soccer (football) in Rome

Romans have a special place in their hearts for football, or soccer, and going to a football game in Rome can be an exciting and unforgettable event. What you need know about football in Rome is as follows:

AS Roma and SS Lazio, two well-known Serie A football teams, are located in Rome. The Stadio Olimpico is where AS Roma plays their home games, while SS Lazio also uses the facility. Due to the heated rivalry and fervent fan bases of both clubs, their games are eagerly anticipated.

Stadio Olimpico: AS Roma and SS Lazio call the Stadio Olimpico their home field. It is the biggest sports arena in Rome. The stadium, which is near the Foro Italico, can hold more than 70,000 people. By going to a game at this legendary location, you may experience the electrifying atmosphere and get completely engrossed in the fervor of Italian football.

Experience on matchday: On game days, the area around the Stadio Olimpico comes alive with supporters wearing their club colors, banners flying, and chanting filling the air. Come early to take in the matchday atmosphere, pick up some street food, and participate in the excitement as people assemble outside the stadium.

Tickets may be bought via the teams' official websites or authorized ticket brokers for the AS Roma and SS Lazio fixtures. It's a good idea to get tickets in advance, particularly for well-known games as they tend to sell out rapidly. To prevent frauds, use caution while purchasing tickets from unreliable sources.

Derby della Capitale: The Rome Derby, commonly known as the Derby della Capitale, is a hotly fought encounter between SS Lazio and AS Roma. The already intense football environment in the city is intensified by this local rivalry. The Rome Derby is an exciting event, but be ready for heightened emotions and more stringent security.

Football Bars and Pubs: There are several sports bars and pubs in Rome that show live football games if you can't get tickets to a game or would rather watch with other fans. These places provide a buzzy environment, large televisions, and a chance to interact with neighborhood football fans.

Football museums: AS Roma and SS Lazio both have specialized museums for football fans who want to learn more about the background and traditions of the game. Both the AS Roma Museum (Museo della Roma) and the SS Lazio Museum (Museo della Lazio) include interactive exhibitions, memorabilia, and trophies that honor the rich histories of the two teams.

Guided Football Tours: You may sign up for guided tours that take you to the stadiums, locker rooms, and other exclusive locations if you're interested in learning more about Rome's football culture from the backstage. These excursions provide insights into the backgrounds and customs of the clubs as well as the workings of Italian football.

Keep in mind to check the match calendar and the websites of the different clubs for the most recent details on ticket availability, match dates, and kickoff times. Attending a football game is an excellent opportunity to fully immerse yourself in the local culture and make lifelong memories, whether you're a die-hard football fan or just want to experience the passion and thrill of the sport in Rome.

Tennis And Golf Clubs

Rome is mostly recognized for its historical and cultural features, but it also provides tennis and golf aficionados with chances. Some renowned tennis and golf facilities in and around Rome are listed below:

Racquet clubs:

Clay courts and first-rate amenities are available at the prominent tennis club Tennis Club Parioli, which is situated in Rome's Parioli area. For players of all ages and ability levels, it provides coaching programs, competitions, and social activities.

Tennis Club Garden: For tennis enthusiasts, Tennis Club Garden offers a tranquil haven close to Villa Borghese. Numerous courts, including clay and artificial grass, a clubhouse, and a welcoming environment are all provided.

One of the most well-known tennis clubs in Rome is Circolo del Tennis Roma, which is renowned for holding major tennis competitions including the Italian Open. It has a variety of amenities, such as hard and clay courts, a swimming pool, and a fitness center.

Clay and hard courts are among the playing surfaces available at Tennis Club Flaminio, which is situated in the Flaminio area. The club offers its members social activities, youth programs, and expert coaching services.

Golf tees:

Golf Club Parco di Roma: This tough 9-hole course is surrounded by ancient Roman ruins and is located inside the Appia Antica Regional Park. The club offers driving range access, golf instruction, and a welcoming clubhouse with a restaurant.

One of the top golfing venues in the area is Golf Club Olgiata, which is located just outside of Rome. It has two 18-hole championship courses that were created by famous golf course architects. Additionally, the club has practice areas, golf lessons, and a clubhouse with food choices.

Marco Simone Golf & Country Club: Marco Simone Golf & Country Club, northeast of Rome, received prominence on a global scale as the 2023 Ryder Cup host venue. The club is a must-visit location for golf aficionados because to its two 18-hole championship courses, a driving range, and first-rate amenities.

Parco di Roma Golf Club: Located in the Veio Regional Park, the scenic 9-hole course at Parco di Roma Golf Club is surrounded by greenery. The club offers practice areas, golf instruction, and a friendly environment for players of all skill levels.

For details on membership, green fees, tee times, and any dress code specifications, it is suggested to consult the individual club websites. These clubs provide fantastic chances to participate in your preferred sports while taking in the picturesque surroundings of Rome, whether you're wanting to play tennis or golf there.

Routes for Jogging and Running

Rome has a number of beautiful paths for jogging and running that let you be active while taking in the city's monuments. Here are a few of Rome's well-liked jogging routes:

The expansive Villa Borghese Gardens provide a peaceful environment for a run. You may explore the many trails in the park and follow the tree-lined pathways. There are flat and incline portions throughout the trail, and you may take in lovely views of the gardens and other landmarks.

Tiber River Path: Joggers often choose to run along the banks of the Tiber River in Rome. Long and generally level, the river walk offers stunning views of the water and well-known bridges including the Ponte Sant'Angelo and Ponte Sisto. You may start close to the Vatican and go either north or south along the river.

Appia Antica Park: With its historic Roman ruins and cobblestone pathways, the Appia Antica Regional Park offers a distinctive jogging experience. Follow the Appian Way, one of the most significant and ancient Roman highways, and take in the serene scenery and interesting sites along the way.

232)

Villa Pamphili Park: The biggest public park in Rome, Villa Doria Pamphilj, provides a roomy, natural backdrop for jogging. You may design your own route across the park using the twisting trails, wide open spaces, and a mixture of flat and steep terrain. While touring the plants and fountains of the park, you may take pleasure in the tranquil ambiance.

Janiculum Hill: The Janiculum Hill offers strenuous exercise and excellent city views for runners. While the climb up might be challenging, the panoramic views of Rome's skyline and well-known sites are worth it. For a picturesque respite, combine your run with a trip to the stunning Fontanone (Janiculum Terrace).

Pincian Hill and Villa Borghese: Start your ascent of the Pincian Hill at Piazza del Popolo while taking in the gardens and shady walks. Continue running through Villa Borghese while varying your path within the park. With chances to take in the beauty of the park and local sights, this route has a variety of uphill and flat areas.

When organizing your run, keep in mind to remain hydrated, wear the proper running attire, and take the weather into account. Additionally, pay attention to how bikes and pedestrians use the roads, especially in busy places. Rome's jogging paths provide you the opportunity to mix exercise with sightseeing, offering a unique approach to take in the beauty and history of the city while keeping active.

Bike Tours and Bicycling

Rome has several bike-friendly routes and tour choices, and biking is a great way to see the city. What you should know about biking and bike excursions in Rome is as follows:

Bike-Friendly Routes: Rome has worked to enhance its bicycle infrastructure, and in certain places, there are lanes and trails just for bikes. Cycling beside the Tiber River, discovering the Appia Antica Regional Park, and traversing the Villa Borghese Gardens are some of the bike-friendly routes. These routes include a variety of beautiful scenery, interesting historical sites, and relatively level terrain.

Biciroma, Rome's bike-sharing program, enables guests to hire bicycles for a certain amount of time. The bikes are simply rented and returned via a smartphone app or at the bike stations themselves, which are dispersed across the city. This is a practical choice for independently touring the city.

Bike Tours: A well-liked method to see Rome's sights while learning about its history and culture is to sign up for a guided bike tour. Popular destinations including the Colosseum, Roman Forum, Vatican City, and other well-known sights are often included in bike excursions. The trip is made interesting and educational by the knowledgeable guides' observations and insights along the route.

Tours on an electric bike are an option if you'd want a more carefree and uncomplicated riding experience. The city's mountainous parts may be more easily navigated while still taking in the views with the use of electric bikes. These trips provide a fun way to go farther and are appropriate for cyclists of different fitness levels.

Safety considerations: It's crucial to pay attention to traffic conditions and abide by local cycling laws while riding in Rome. Helmet usage, hand signals for turns, and following traffic regulations are all recommended. Be wary of people on foot, particularly in congested places, and always lock your bike up tightly when stopping.

Self-guided Exploration: Renting a bike from a nearby bike store is an alternative if you want to go on your own. A variety of bikes, including city bikes, mountain bikes, and even electric bikes, are available for hire at a number of locations throughout Rome. You may plan your own itinerary and explore the city at your own speed using a map or GPS.

When deciding whether to go on a bike tour or hire a bike, weigh the time, cost, and needs of each choice. It's also advised to examine the weather and choose a convenient time of day to go riding. By riding a bike about Rome, you can take in the city's splendor, negotiate its winding streets, and find hidden jewels while soaking in the vibrant spirit of the Eternal City.

Sports on the Tiber River's waterways

While water sports are not often associated with the Tiber River in Rome, there are a handful that you may partake in there. The Tiber River offers the following opportunities for water sports:

Renting a kayak or a canoe will allow you to paddle down the Tiber River while seeing Rome from a new angle. You can explore the river at your own leisure thanks to rental businesses that provide equipment and guided trips.

Stand-Up Paddleboarding (SUP): The Tiber River provides a distinctive backdrop to attempt this pastime, which is growing in popularity in Rome. Take a paddleboard rental and explore the tranquil river while taking in the urban setting. For novices or those seeking a guided experience, SUP courses and excursions are also offered.

Rowing: You may join a rowing club or group that uses the Tiber River if you have previous expertise in the sport. These clubs provide rowers the chance to practice, compete, and take part in rowing events. The Tiber River is a tranquil and beautiful place to row, particularly in the early morning or late afternoon.

River Cruises: Although not a conventional water sport, enjoying a river cruise on the Tiber is a well-liked tourist activity. Take a leisurely boat trip down the river to see Rome's well-known attractions from a new angle. There are other types of cruises, such as dinner cruises and sightseeing trips.

It's crucial to remember that, depending on the time of year and regional circumstances, water activities on the Tiber River may only be sometimes available or subject to certain restrictions. For the most recent information on safety precautions, equipment rental, and any necessary permissions or licenses, it is best to contact local tour operators or rental businesses.

Additionally, pay attention to the river's currents and heed any safety advice given. Always put your safety first, and make sure you have the knowledge and expertise required for the water activity you've selected.

Fitness Facilities and Gyms

There are several gyms and fitness facilities spread all around Rome if you want to keep up your exercise program while you're there. Here are a few possibilities for gyms and fitness facilities in Rome:

Virgin Active: With several sites throughout Rome, Virgin Active is a well-known fitness business. They include a variety of fitness equipment, group workout programs, swimming pools, and other perks like saunas and steam rooms.

Technogym Wellness Center: Technogym is an Italian company that makes workout equipment and runs its own wellness facilities. They provide cutting-edge facilities, customized fitness plans, and a selection of training sessions.

Holmes Place: Another well-known fitness business with multiple facilities in Rome is Holmes Place. They include wellness facilities including spas and relaxation rooms, as well as contemporary gym equipment, group fitness programs, personal trainer services, and other services.

The Centro Sportivo Farnesina is a sports facility that offers a variety of amenities, including a gym, indoor and outdoor swimming pools, tennis courts, and numerous sports fields. It is situated in the Prati area.

Fitprime provides a variety of high-intensity exercises, functional training, and specialist programs including Pilates, yoga, and cycling. Fitprime is a boutique fitness center in Rome.

Local Municipal Gyms: Local municipal gyms, or "Palestre Comunali," are available in many Rome areas. These facilities are often inexpensive and include basic exercise equipment and fitness programs.

It's vital to keep in mind that certain gyms could demand a membership or day pass to enter; as a result, it's advised to visit their websites or get in touch with them personally to learn more about costs and scheduling. Additionally, services and hours of operation may differ, so it's best to enquire in advance about any particular needs or limitations.

240)

When attending a gym or fitness facility, keep in mind to carry suitable training gear, a towel, and a water bottle.

Sports Competitions And Events

Rome has several sporting events and contests all year long that represent a variety of athletic specialties. You may take part in or attend the following well-known sporting events while visiting Rome:

Soccer: Rome is the home of two renowned soccer teams, A.S. Romano and S.S. Lazio. The Stadio Olimpico, which also holds international football games and other athletic events, is where you can watch their games. Sports fans must attend a live football game to experience the electrifying atmosphere.

Rugby: The Azzurri, the Italian national rugby team, sometimes plays matches in Rome. The thrilling rugby matches involving Italy or club teams may be seen at the Stadio Olimpico or Stadio Flaminio.

Tennis: The Internazionali BNL d'Italia is a yearly tennis competition held in Rome as a part of the ATP and WTA Tour. On the clay courts of the Foro Italico, top-ranked tennis players from all over the globe participate, giving fans the chance to see elite tennis action.

Athletics: The Golden Gala Pietro Mennea is a track and field competition that takes place every year in Rome. Top international competitors compete in a variety of events, including sprints, long jumps, shot puts, and others. The Olimpico Stadium or the Stadio dei Marmi are the venues for the event.

Marathons and Running Events: Throughout the year, Rome plays home to a number of marathons and running competitions. The Maratona di Roma (Rome Marathon) is a well-known race that draws participants from all over the globe. The Rome Half Marathon and several charity races are additional running competitions.

Cycling: Rome sometimes serves as a venue for illustrious cycling competitions like the Giro d'Italia. You may see the excitement of professional cyclists in action as the city's streets and environs serve as the setting for exhilarating cycling championships.

These are just a few instances of the sporting events and contests that are held in Rome. It is advised to look into the event schedules, ticket prices, and particular dates for any event you want to attend. Being present at a live sporting event may be an exhilarating and unforgettable experience that allows you to fully feel the passion and fervor of the athletic world.

SUSTAINABLE AND RESPONSIBLE TRAVEL

Environmentally Friendly Lodging Options

There are several ecologically responsible hotels and motels that stress sustainability and lessen their ecological impact if you're seeking eco-friendly lodging alternatives in Rome. Following are a few eco-friendly lodging choices in Rome:

The Beehive is a well-known eco-friendly hostel close to Termini Station. It provides organic, vegetarian, and vegan breakfast alternatives and is dedicated to sustainability. Throughout all aspects of its operations, the hostel supports recycling, energy efficiency, and environmentally responsible activities.

Hotel Domus Sessoriana: This hotel is located on the grounds of the Basilica of St. John Lateran in an ancient edifice. It is renowned for its eco-friendly policies, which include recycling programs, the usage of energy-efficient equipment, and organic food alternatives.

Hotel Villa San Pio is a family-run establishment that places a strong emphasis on eco-friendly procedures. It is tucked away in the peaceful Aventine Hill area. The hotel offers eco-friendly facilities, a lovely garden, and solar electricity.

Hotel All Time Relais & Sport: This hotel, which is close to Villa Doria Pamphili, blends contemporary luxury with eco-friendly principles. It has LED lighting, energy-efficient technology, and environmentally friendly toiletries. Additionally, the hotel provides services for athletes including a fitness facility.

The NH Hotels company is dedicated to environmentally friendly measures, and the Rome hotel is no exception. The hotel places a strong emphasis on waste minimization, energy saving, and eco-friendly guest experiences.

Listings on Airbnb that are eco-friendly: Rome has a variety of eco-friendly lodging options. These listings often have an emphasis on environmental design, energy efficiency, and sustainability.

Check for certifications like LEED (Leadership in Energy and Environmental Design) or see whether a hotel has embraced particular sustainability programs while looking for eco-friendly lodging. You may also ask them about how they handle garbage, how they utilize renewable energy, how they save water, and if they provide organic food.

While enjoying your trip to Rome, you can support ecologically friendly activities by staying in environmentally friendly accommodations.

Rome's Recycling and Waste Management

Recycling and garbage management are crucial components of fostering environmental sustainability and minimizing the negative effects on the ecology of the city of Rome. Here are some details about Rome's recycling and trash disposal procedures:

Rome has a recycling program in place, and both locals and tourists are urged to take part. For various recyclable items, such as paper, plastic, glass, and metal, the city supplies several containers. These bins, which are often color-coded, may be seen all over the city, at places like homes, parks, and next to businesses.

Search for the recycling marks on packaging, which designate the proper disposal container. Typically, the symbols are accompanied by language that describes the substance (such as plastic or glass) or uses color coding to denote various recycling categories.

Separate rubbish Collection: Rome encourages separate rubbish collection in addition to recycling. This entails separating organic garbage from regular waste (such as food leftovers and yard debris). For the disposal of organic waste, several locations provide special containers or composting systems. Separating organic waste enables composting or other methods of managing it, which helps keep it out of landfills.

Garbage Disposal Rules: It's crucial to abide by Rome's garbage disposal rules. Refrain from leaving rubbish behind or polluting public places. To guarantee effective waste management, abide by the authorized garbage collection times and disposal procedures.

Garbage-to-electricity Facilities: Non-recyclable garbage is converted into electricity in waste-to-energy facilities in Rome. These facilities contribute to energy generation via incineration or other waste-to-energy conversion techniques while assisting in reducing the amount of garbage that ends up in landfills.

Recycling Facilities: Residents may bring certain trash kinds to Rome's recycling facilities for appropriate disposal or recycling. Electronic garbage, batteries, textiles, and hazardous materials are all accepted at these facilities. They provide a practical and sensible option to get rid of things that aren't suitable for normal recycling containers.

Public Awareness and Education: To encourage recycling and trash management practices, the city of Rome runs public awareness campaigns and educational initiatives. These programs seek to increase public awareness of the value of recycling, trash reduction, and appropriate garbage disposal among locals and tourists.

It's important to note that rules and procedures for garbage disposal in various Rome areas and municipalities may differ. To guarantee adherence to regional waste management procedures, it is advised to review the detailed recommendations issued by local authorities or to speak with lodging providers.

You may aid in Rome's overall sustainability efforts and lessen the environmental effect of trash creation by taking part in recycling programs, sorting rubbish, and being attentive of proper waste disposal.

Green Spaces and Parks

There are several parks and green areas in Rome where locals and tourists may rest, take in the scenery, and participate in outdoor activities. Here are some of Rome's prominent parks and green spaces:

One of Rome's biggest parks, Villa Borghese, provides a calm haven away from the busy city. Large lawns, lovely gardens, a lake with rowboats, fountains, and a number of museums and art galleries are among its highlights. Visitors have the option of renting bicycles or enjoying a leisurely walk while admiring the natural beauty.

The biggest manicured public park in Rome is called Villa Doria Pamphili, and it is situated in the Monteverde district. Its 180 hectares are covered with beautiful vegetation, well-kept gardens, walking trails, and a lake. It's the perfect location for picnics, running, or just unwinding in the great outdoors.

The Park of the Aqueducts (Parco degli Acquedotti) is a beautiful outdoor recreation area that has historic Roman aqueducts. The historical aqueducts that previously provided water to the city may be seen as visitors stroll or ride bicycles along the routes.

The Appian Way Park, also known as the Appia Antica Regional Park, follows the route of the historic Appian Way and offers a tranquil setting for strolling, cycling, and visiting Roman antiquities. Roman villas, catacombs, and ancient graves are scattered throughout the park.

The Orto Botanico di Roma (Rome Botanical Garden) is a paradise for those who are interested in plants. It is situated on the slopes of the Janiculum Hill. It has a huge variety of plant species, including rare flowers, medicinal plants, and exotic trees. The garden's trails are perfect for leisurely strolls where visitors may take in the tranquil atmosphere.

The Aventine Hill's Parco Savello (Orange Garden) provides breathtaking vistas of Rome, including the Tiber River and St. Peter's Basilica. The park is a well-liked place to unwind and take in the sunset since it is full with aromatic orange trees.

250)

Villa Ada: There is plenty of room for outdoor activities in this sizable park in Rome's north. It has a lake, walking routes, picnic places, and even a small amphitheater. It also has some forested parts. It's a nice location to get away from the bustle of the city.

Rome's parks and natural areas provide chances for leisure, relaxation, and getting back to nature. Rome's green areas have something for everyone to enjoy, whether you're searching for a quiet getaway, a beautiful stroll, or a location to enjoy outdoor sports.

ITINERARY SUGGESTIONS

Rome in 3 Days: Must-See Attractions and Highlights

Rome's highlights and must-see sights may be covered in three days if you have that much time to spend there. To help you make the most of your time, consider the following itinerary:

Day 1:

Morning: Start the day with Rome's most recognizable site, the Colosseum. Discover the intriguing history of the historic amphitheater.

Visit the Roman Forum in the afternoon, which is close to the Colosseum. This archaeological complex, which is full with the remains of temples, governmental structures, and public areas, served as the hub of ancient Roman society.

Evening: Take a walk through the quaint Trastevere area. Dine at one of the numerous genuine Roman trattorias there, and take pleasure in the city's lively ambiance and winding cobblestone alleyways.

Day 2:

Morning: Visit St. Peter's Basilica before seeing Vatican City. Take in its magnificence, explore the Vatican Grottoes, and scale the dome for sweeping vistas of the city.

Afternoon: Explore the Vatican Museums, which include a noteworthy collection of works of art and artifacts from antiquity. Don't miss the breathtaking Sistine Chapel, which has famous murals by Michelangelo.

Evening: Visit Piazza Navona, a gorgeous piazza with magnificent Baroque buildings, fountains, and outdoor cafes. Enjoy street entertainers, go for a leisurely walk, and have dinner at a welcoming restaurant.

Day 3:

Visit the Pantheon in the morning. It is a magnificently preserved Roman temple. Examine the inside and take in the stunning architecture.

Afternoon: Explore the historic center's quaint streets while stopping at the Trevi Fountain, the Spanish Steps, and Piazza di Spagna. Enjoy some gelato from a neighboring gelateria while admiring the splendor of these well-known locations.

Evening: Cap off your day with a dynamic nighttime scene in the vivacious Campo de' Fiori, a busy area with a bustling market throughout the day. Dine at a neighborhood trattoria and take in the bustling ambiance.

Spend some time taking leisurely strolls, enjoying people-watching at outdoor cafés, and discovering Rome's hidden gems. Rome is a city best explored at a slow pace, so be open to unplanned discoveries and immerse yourself in its rich history and lively culture. This itinerary does, however, cover the key landmarks.

Rome in Seven Days: A Comprehensive Tour

Rome may be thoroughly explored if you have seven days to spare, enabling you to learn more about the city's past, present, and secret attractions. Here is a recommended schedule to help you make the most of your week:

Day 1:

Early in the morning, start your tour in Vatican City. Visit the Vatican Grottoes, explore St. Peter's Basilica, and go to the top of the dome for sweeping views.
Afternoon: Take the opportunity to see the Vatican Museums, which include the Sistine Chapel and many other works of art.
Evening: Take a leisurely stroll along the Tiber River before dining at a nearby riverfront establishment.

Day 2:

Morning: Explore the Colosseum and Roman Forum to get a glimpse of ancient Rome.

Investigate the historic amphitheater and the old city's remains.
Visit Palatine Hill in the afternoon to explore the sizable remains and take in the mesmerizing vistas of Rome.
Evening: Take in the bustling energy of the Trastevere district. Enjoy the authentic Roman food and the bohemian atmosphere while strolling through its lovely streets.

Day 3:

Morning: Start at the Pantheon and immerse yourself in the historical district. Admire its wonderful architecture and discover the neighborhood.
Visit the Trevi Fountain, the Spanish Steps, and Piazza Navona in the afternoon. Enjoy some gelato from one of the neighboring gelaterias while taking your time to see the splendor of these famous sites.
Evening: Take in the lively ambiance of Campo de' Fiori, which is well-known for its busy market during the day and frenetic nightlife at night. Enjoy supper while taking in the atmosphere of the area.

Day 4:

255)

Morning: Tour the quaint Monti area. Discover its fashionable shops, quaint streets, and Basilica of Santa Maria Maggiore.

Afternoon: Visit the Appian Way Regional Park to see the catacombs, old Roman road, and other historical monuments.

Evening: Spend a peaceful evening strolling in one of Rome's lovely gardens, such as Villa Borghese or Villa Doria Pamphili.

Day 5:

Morning: Take a tour of Testaccio, a bustling district famous for its food market and regional cuisine from Rome. Visit the Museum of Contemporary Art (MACRO) and take in the vibrant atmosphere of the area.

Afternoon: Visit the well preserved ancient Roman harbor city of Ostia Antica. Discover the amphitheater, baths, and market square among its remains.

Evening: Enjoy the nightlife in the hip Ostiense neighborhood, which is renowned for its street art, bars, and cultural establishments.

Day 6:

Visit the lovely Aventine Hill in the morning and take in the tranquility of the Orange

Garden (Parco Savello). View Rome in its entirety from this vantage point.

Explore the MAXXI - National Museum of 21st Century Arts, which is devoted to modern art and architecture, in the afternoon.

Evening: Savor the tastes of the city by indulging in a classic Roman meal at a nearby trattoria.

Day 7:

Morning: Travel to Tivoli for the day and see the magnificent Villa d'Este and Hadrian's Villa. Explore the stunning fountains, gardens, and ruins.

Afternoon: Travel back to Rome and spend the day exploring the quaint streets and boutiques of the affluent Prati quarter.

Evening: Enjoy a wonderful goodbye meal at a rooftop restaurant to end your week in Rome while taking in breath-blowing views of the city.

This route offers a thorough tour of Rome.

Off the Beaten Path Itinerary

Here are a few interesting itineraries to think about if you want to experience Rome off the main path and away from the typical tourist crowds:

Neighborhoods and Hidden Gems:

Discover the excellent Roman-Jewish food and rich history of the Jewish Ghetto.
Learn about the less well-known area of Garbatella, which is renowned for its unique architecture and small-town charm.
Explore the Coppedè district, which is renowned for its colorful and unique architectural design.
Visit the Quartiere Coppedè, a hidden treasure with magnificent Art Nouveau structures and a distinctive ambiance.
Rome's history extends beyond the Colosseum.

Discover lesser-known historical monuments like the Cestius Pyramid and the Baths of Caracalla.
Visit Rome's Catacombs, a network of subterranean tombs with intriguing historical and theological importance.
Explore the striking remains of Roman aqueducts including the Aqua Virgo and Aqua Claudia.

258)

Visit the well-preserved remains of the ancient Roman harbor city of Ostia Antica on a day excursion.

Gardens & Parks:

Among Rome's biggest parks, Villa Ada is renowned for its picturesque vistas, lakes, and picnic spaces. Spend the day there.

Investigate the lovely grounds of Villa Torlonia, a collection of antique structures and architectural wonders.

Discover the huge variety of plant species and serene environment in the Orto Botanico (Botanical Garden).

Visit the Appian Way Regional Park where you may picnic, go cycling, or just stroll along the historic Roman route.

Museums and the Arts

At the Mattatoio, a former slaughterhouse turned cultural hub with art exhibits, concerts, and workshops, learn about modern art.

Visit the Centrale Montemartini, a quirky museum located in a former power plant, which offers a unique fusion of antiquated sculptures and modern equipment.

Explore the Museo di Roma in Trastevere, which uses artwork and antiques to illustrate the neighborhood's history and culture.

Learn more about the Museo delle Anime del Purgatorio (Museum of the Souls of Purgatory), a modest but fascinating museum devoted to the afterlife.

gastronomic delights

Take a culinary tour of Testaccio, a neighborhood renowned for its local markets, authentic Roman cuisine, and destinations for foodies.

Visit the farmer's market, Mercato di Campagna Amica del Circo Massimo, where you may sample and buy handcrafted goods and fresh local vegetables.

Discover the fashionable bars, inviting restaurants, and delicious street food choices in the Pigneto neighborhood, which is well-known for its thriving food and drink scene.

Learn about the origins and workmanship of Italian gelato at the Gelato Museum Carpigiani, a short distance from Rome.

These off-the-beaten-track itineraries will enable you to discover Rome's lesser-known features, giving you a distinctive and genuine experience of the city. Plan your trips in advance since certain places may have restricted hours or demand reservations.

Options For Day Trips And Extended Tours

There are several wonderful day trip alternatives and lengthy excursions available if you have additional time while visiting Rome and wish to go beyond the city. Here are some recommendations:

the Mount Vesuvius and Pompeii:

Take a day excursion to Pompeii, an ancient city that was preserved by layers of volcanic ash after Mount Vesuvius' explosion in 79 AD.
Discover the impressively preserved remains of Pompeii, including the Forum, the amphitheater, and the well-known human figure plaster casts.
Hike to the crater of Mount Vesuvius for stunning panoramic views of the surroundings.
Tivoli: Hadrian's Villa and Villa d'Este:

Visit the charming village of Tivoli, which is close to Rome.
Discover the magnificent Villa d'Este, known for its spectacular Renaissance terraces, gardens, and fountains.
Visit the stunning archaeological monument known as Hadrian's Villa (Villa Adriana),

which displays the splendor of the ancient home of the Roman Emperor Hadrian.

A Day Trip to Renaissance City, Florence:

From Rome, take a fast train to Florence, where you may spend the day sightseeing.
Visit well-known sites including the Ponte Vecchio, the Uffizi Gallery, and the Duomo.
Take in the Renaissance-era architecture and art while indulging on gelato and food from Tuscany.

Oriente Antico:

Visit Ostia Antica, a former harbor of the Roman Empire situated close to the Tiber River's mouth.
Investigate the astonishingly well-preserved remains, which include an amphitheater, hot springs, and historic homes.
Explore the historic buildings and streets to learn more about everyday life in ancient Rome.

Orvieto:

Visit the lovely Umbrian hilltop town of Orvieto on a day trip.
Enjoy the majestic Orvieto Cathedral's breathtaking exterior and detailed interior.

Discover the tunnels and caverns left by the ancient Etruscans in the subterranean city.

Eat delectable Umbrian food and sample regional wines.

Coast of the Amalfi:

Set off on a lengthy excursion to the spectacular Amalfi Coast, which is renowned for its beautiful cliffside villages and azure seas.

Take a trip to Positano, Amalfi, and Ravello, three beautiful cities.

Take in the breathtaking scenery, unwind on stunning beaches, and indulge in the area's world-famous seafood and lemon-infused cuisine.

The countryside of Tuscany

On a day excursion from Rome, see the beautiful Tuscan countryside.

Visit quaint cities like Pienza, Siena, and San Gimignano.

Enjoy this lovely area's undulating hills, wineries, and historic sites.

Enjoy local wines and indulge in some Tuscan food.

These extended excursions and day trip alternatives provide visitors the opportunity to see Italy's diverse history, fine art, and scenic beauty outside of Rome. Every traveler's tastes may be satisfied, whether they are drawn to Renaissance art, old ruins, or breathtaking vistas. To make the most of your stay in Italy, plan your day excursions and longer tours with consideration for time, logistics, and transit alternatives.

Thematic and Seasonal Itineraries

Consider the following seasonal and theme itineraries to offer more depth and thematic inquiry to your trip to Rome:

Springtime Pleasures

Discover Rome's vivid parks and gardens, including Villa Borghese and the Orto Botanico, as they come to life with bright blossoms.
Attend Easter festivities and take in the city's religious customs and processions.
Visit the Vatican in the spring when religious activities and festivities are more prevalent.
Summer vacations:

During the hot summer months, take advantage of the lively atmosphere at Rome's outdoor cafés, gelatarias, and piazzas.

For a tranquil respite from the heat of the city, take a refreshing swim at one of Austria's neighboring beaches or go exploring in the Roman countryside.

Attend outdoor performances, festivals, and movie screenings that are held all throughout the city.

Harvest in autumn:

Discover Rome's culinary scene in the fall, when the city's bounty of seasonal foods and fresh vegetables is on display.

To enjoy the flavors of the fall harvest, explore the neighborhood markets and take part in culinary excursions.

Visit Castelli Romani or Frascati, two local wine-producing areas, to partake in wine tastings and vineyard excursions.

Holiday Magic

Spend the Christmas season in Rome and take in all the festivities.

Shop for distinctive presents and decorations at renowned Christmas markets like the one in Piazza Navona.

The midnight Mass at St. Peter's Basilica is one of the Christmas concerts and shows that you should attend.

Visit the city's exquisitely illuminated streets and squares, where you can see the magnificent Christmas tree that stands in front of the Colosseum.

Roman Antiquity Rediscovered:

By seeing the Colosseum, Roman Forum, and Palatine IIill, you may delve deeply into Rome's extensive historical past.

Investigate lesser-known ancient monuments like the Domus Aurea (Nero's Golden House) and the Basilica of San Clemente's basement levels.

Attend classes or guided tours that highlight the art, architecture, and way of life of the ancient Romans.

Baroque and Renaissance splendor

Visit museums like the Galleria Borghese, Capitoline Museums, and Vatican Museums to learn about Rome's Renaissance and Baroque creative masterpieces.

Discover the cathedrals and palaces that include works of art by Michelangelo, Caravaggio, and Bernini.

Visit historical locations like the Church of Sant'Ivo alla Sapienza or the Teatro dell'Opera to see classical music concerts or opera performances.

Foodie Journey

Explore Italian cuisine by enrolling in cooking lessons or culinary excursions that highlight the regional tastes and age-old recipes of Rome.

Investigate the city's different gastronomic neighborhoods, including Trastevere and Testaccio, which are renowned for their traditional Roman cuisine and magnets for foodies.

To experience the many tastes of Rome's gastronomic culture, visit regional markets, specialized food stores, and wine bars.

Rome offers many unique experiences and cultural landmarks, so you may completely immerse yourself in them by planning your schedule according to the seasons or certain themes. To take full use of these seasonal and themed itineraries, organize your vacation taking into account the season and your specific interests.

Personalizing Your Visit to Rome

To get the most out of your vacation and adapt to your own interests, it's crucial to personalize your Rome experience. Here are some suggestions for personalizing your visit to Rome:

Determine Your Interests: Choose the elements of Rome's history, art, culture, and gastronomy that most interest you. Are you a fan of history who is curious about ancient Rome? Or maybe you're an art lover anxious to see the city's galleries and museums. You can prioritize your tasks and use your time more effectively if you are aware of your hobbies.

Make a customized schedule that matches your interests and preferences by planning according to your choices. Highlight the must-see monuments and sites that match your preferences while giving you the freedom to explore off-the-beaten-path areas or partake in locally appealing activities.

Consult travel forums and blogs or talk to locals to receive insider tips for undiscovered treasures, underrated sights, and genuine eating experiences. Locals may provide insightful advice and direct you toward lesser-known yet distinctive features of Rome.

Consider attending Guided Tours: Consider attending guided tours if you want a customized experience or want in-depth information about certain locations. Pick excursions based on your interests, such as walking tours with an emphasis on art, cuisine, or history. These might help you comprehend and appreciate Rome's rich history and culture.

Embrace the Local Culture: Participate in Customary Activities or Local Events to Fully Immerse Yourself in the Local Culture. This can include taking a culinary lesson, picking up a few fundamental Italian words and phrases, or conversing with locals in markets and coffee shops. Accepting the local culture will enhance your trip and provide special memories.

Balance Must-See monuments with Hidden Gems: Rome is full with famous monuments, but don't skip the lesser-known attractions that provide a more personal and genuine experience. Include a variety of locations on your schedule, such as lesser-known districts, regional markets, and parks that provide a look into Romans' everyday lives in addition to well-known attractions like the Colosseum and Vatican City.

Prioritize Quality Over Quantity: There are many attractions in Rome, but attempting to visit them all in a short amount of time might be exhausting. Focus on fewer attractions and give yourself enough time to really enjoy and investigate each location to place quality above quantity. This will make the event more fun and meaningful.

Remember that you may adjust your Rome experience to suit your interests and tastes. It's about designing a trip that speaks to you and has an impact on you. You may make your trip to Rome a genuinely unique and memorable experience by taking into account your hobbies, finding out local insights, and embracing the local culture.

Multi-Destination Itineraries: Beyond Rome

There are many fascinating locations in Italy that may be coupled with your visit to make a multi-destination itinerary if you have more time to explore than just Rome. Here are a few well-liked choices:

Florence: Easily accessible from Rome, Florence is a must-visit city known for its Renaissance art and architecture. Discover well-known locations including the Ponte Vecchio, Uffizi Gallery, and the Duomo. Eat delectable Tuscan fare while strolling along the Arno River.

Discover the allure of Venice, a city known for its gondolas, canals, and quaint alleys. Visit the Doge's Palace, St. Mark's Square, and the famous Rialto Bridge. Enjoy Venetian cuisine while riding in a gondola in a romantic setting.

Discover the breathtaking Amalfi Coast, a stretch of coastline with charming villages built on cliffs overlooking the azure Mediterranean Sea. Visit Positano, Amalfi, and Ravello to take in the mesmerizing scenery, delectable seafood, and relaxing beach time.

Explore Tuscany's picturesque landscape, which is renowned for its rolling hills, wineries, and quaint towns. Visit the famous Leaning Tower of Pisa, the Chianti wine region, and Siena, a historic town. Take part in farm-to-table dining and wine tastings while experiencing the culture of Tuscany.

Naples and Pompeii: Travel to Naples to take in the energetic city life, savor real Neapolitan pizza, and see the National Archaeological Museum. Visit the remaining remnants of this once vibrant Roman city by taking a day trip to Pompeii.

Sicily: Visit the island of Sicily for a more unusual experience. Discover Palermo's rich history, awe at the Greek remains in Agrigento, and climb Mount Etna, the biggest active volcano in Europe. Enjoy some Sicilian food and get to know the island's fascinating culture.

Cinque Terre: Explore the vibrant seaside towns that make up the UNESCO World Heritage site of Cinque Terre. soak a leisurely boat trip to soak in the spectacular vistas, or hike along the lovely pathways that link the five settlements. Try local wines and delicious seafood in the quaint village squares.

Consider the length of your vacation, your transportation alternatives, and your particular interests when creating a multi-destination itinerary. It's best to allot enough time at each location to really investigate and enjoy their distinctive attractions. Rome combined with other Italian locations will provide you a varied and rewarding travel experience, whether you decide to concentrate on art and history, coastline beauty, or gastronomic pleasures.

Car Rental Businesses

There are several trustworthy vehicle rental agencies to choose from when hiring a car in Rome. Here are a few reputable automobile rental businesses with locations in Rome:

Hertz: A well-known automobile rental business with a significant presence in Rome is Hertz. They have several rental facilities across the city, notably at Termini Train Station and Fiumicino Airport, and they provide a large range of automobiles.

Avis: Another well-known rental vehicle business operating in Rome is Avis. For various needs and tastes, they provide a variety of automobiles. The city is home to a number of Avis rental sites, including those at Termini Train Station and Fiumicino Airport.

273)

The reputable automobile rental company Europcar provides a range of cars to meet various demands. There are several rental outlets for them in Rome, including the Termini Train Station, Ciampino Airport, and Fiumicino Airport.

Budget: The company is renowned for its dependable service and affordable costs. They are present in Romc, having rental stations at the airports of Fiumicino, Ciampino, and Termini.

Sixt: Sixt is a worldwide provider of automobile rentals having a location in Rome. They have several rental stations across the city, notably at the Fiumicino Airport and Termini Train Station, and they provide a variety of automobiles.

The well-known vehicle rental firm Enterprise has a location in Rome. They provide a range of automobiles and have rental outlets at Ciampino Airport, Termini Train Station, and Fiumicino Airport.

Before making a reservation, it is advised to compare costs, read reviews, and research the terms and conditions of each vehicle rental business. The necessity for an International Driving Permit (IDP) for license holders from outside the European Union is another thing to be aware of while driving in Italy.

Dos and Don'ts

It is good to be aware of certain dos and don'ts while visiting Rome in order to have a courteous and pleasurable trip. Here are some key principles to bear in mind:

Dos:

When visiting churches and other religious buildings, dress accordingly. In order to show respect, cover your knees and shoulders.
While visiting the city, have a copy of your passport and identification with you.
Try to pick up a few fundamental Italian words and phrases, such as salutations and expressions of politeness. The effort is appreciated by the locals, and it might improve your relationships.
Do exercise caution with your possessions and keep an eye out for pickpockets, particularly in

busy tourist locations. In busy areas, keep your valuables locked up and stay on the lookout.

Do sample the regional fare, which includes real Italian pizza, pasta, gelato, and espresso. Rome has a vast variety of delectable foods that must not be missed.

When feasible, explore the city on foot. It is advisable to wander around Rome's old center to find hidden jewels and take in the ambiance.

To avoid crowds and lengthy lines, visit popular sites and attractions early in the day. You may save time and have a more enjoyable trip by making plans in advance and buying your tickets online.

Respect the regional traditions and customs. Be kind and respectful in your encounters since Italians are renowned for their warmth and friendliness.

Don'ts:

Avoid engaging with street merchants offering fake items or falling for frauds. Be wary of anybody attempting to divert your attention or providing uninvited aid.

Validate your public transportation ticket right now. To avoid penalties, verify your ticket at the authorized machines if you're using the bus, tram, or metro.

Avoid tossing money into old fountains, such as the Trevi Fountain. To harm or pollute these famous sites is against the law and disrespectful.

Don't limit your transportation options to cabs. Although they might be useful, cabs can sometimes be costly and prone to excessive traffic. Whenever possible, try to walk or use public transit.

Avoid eating at tourist trap establishments close to popular sites. For genuine and affordable food alternatives, explore the surrounding areas.

Don't undervalue the amount of time needed to see all of Rome's sights. Make a smart plan for your trip, providing enough time to take in each location without feeling hurried.

Remember to check the attractions' and museums' opening times. Some businesses may have set closure dates or less hours on some days of the week.

If you're driving in Rome, don't forget to verify your parking ticket. Fines may apply if you don't verify your ticket.

You may explore Rome with respect, awareness, and a deeper understanding for the city's rich culture and history by adhering to these dos and don'ts.

Conclusion

Rome is a fascinating city with a colorful history, stunning architecture, and a complex culture. Rome has plenty to offer everyone, whether you're a history buff, an art connoisseur, a gourmet, or just looking for an authentic travel experience. The city is a treasure trove waiting to be discovered, with well-known attractions like the Colosseum and the Vatican City as well as lovely districts and undiscovered jewels.

You have access to a thorough table of contents for this comprehensive travel guide to Rome that covers a variety of topics related to your trip, such as history, attractions, eating, shopping, transit, and more. You may now customize your schedule depending on your interests and preferences thanks to the insights it has provided about the city's well-known landmarks, districts, and cultural activities.

Be sure to respect the city's history and traditions, adopt local practices if possible, and try to mingle with the amiable residents. The greatest way to explore Rome is to immerse yourself in its culture, enjoy its food, and walk through its streets.

This book has given you the knowledge you need to make the most of your stay in Rome, whether you have a few days or a week to spend there. So prepare for an extraordinary vacation in Rome by packing your luggage, exploring the city's rich history, and indulging in its delectable cuisine. Bon voyage!

Printed in Great Britain
by Amazon

25427765R00155